The Essential Martin Luther

The Large Catechism of Martin Luther
Selected Sermons of Martin Luther
Martin Luther's Ninety-Five Theses

The Essential Martin Luther
by Martin Luther

The Large Catechism of Martin Luther

Table of Contents

Preface

A Christian, Profitable, and Necessary Preface and Faithful, Earnest Exhortation of Dr. Martin Luther to All Christians, but Especially to All Pastors and Preachers, that They Should Daily Exercise Themselves in the Catechism, which is a Short Summary and Epitome of the Entire Holy Scriptures, and that They May Always Teach the Same.

We have no slight reasons for treating the Catechism so constantly [in sermons] and for both desiring and beseeching others to teach it, since we see to our sorrow that many pastors and preachers are very negligent in this, and slight both their office and this teaching; some from great and high art [giving their mind, as they imagine, to much higher matters], but others from sheer laziness and care for their paunches, assuming no other relation to this business than if they were pastors and preachers for their bellies' sake, and had nothing to do but to [spend and] consume their emoluments as long as they live, as they have been accustomed to do under the Papacy.

And although they have now everything that they are to preach and teach placed before them so abundantly, clearly, and easily, in so many [excellent and] helpful books, and the true Sermones per se loquentes, Dormi secure, Paratos et Thesauros, as they were called in former times; yet they are not so godly and honest as to buy these books, or even when they have them, to look at them or read them. Alas! they are altogether shameful gluttons and servants of their own bellies who ought to be more properly swineherds and dog-tenders than care-takers of souls and pastors.

And now that they are delivered from the unprofitable and burdensome babbling of the Seven Canonical Hours, oh, that, instead thereof, they would only, morning, noon, and evening, read a page or two in the Catechism, the Prayer-book, the New Testament, or elsewhere in the Bible, and pray the Lord's Prayer for themselves and their parishioners, so that they might render, in return, honor and thanks to the Gospel, by which they have been delivered from burdens and troubles so manifold, and might feel a little shame because like pigs and dogs they retain no more of the Gospel than such a lazy, pernicious, shameful, carnal liberty! For, alas! as it is, the common people regard the Gospel altogether too lightly, and we accomplish nothing extraordinary even though we use all diligence. What, then, will be achieved if we shall be negligent and lazy as we were under the Papacy?

To this there is added the shameful vice and secret infection of security and satiety, that is, that many regard the Catechism as a poor, mean teaching, which they can read through at one time, and then immediately know it, throw the book into a corner, and be ashamed, as it were, to read in it again.

Yea, even among the nobility there may be found some louts and scrimps, who declare that there is no longer any need either of pastors or preachers; that we have everything in books, and every one can easily learn it by himself; and so they are content to let the parishes decay and become desolate, and pastors and preachers to suffer distress and hunger a plenty, just as it becomes crazy Germans to do. For we Germans have such disgraceful people, and must endure them.

But for myself I say this: I am also a doctor and preacher, yea, as learned and experienced as all those may be who have such presumption and security; yet I do as a child who is being taught the Catechism, and every morning, and whenever I have time, I read and say, word for word, the Ten Commandments, the Creed, the Lord's Prayer, the Psalms, etc. And I must still read and study daily, and yet I cannot master it as I wish, but must remain a child and pupil of the Catechism, and am glad so to remain. And yet these delicate, fastidious fellows would with one reading promptly be doctors above all doctors, know everything and be in need of nothing. Well, this, too, is indeed a sure sign that they despise both their office and the souls of the people, yea, even God and His Word. They do not have to fall, they are already fallen all too horribly, they would need to become children, and begin to learn their alphabet, which they imagine that they have long since outgrown.

Therefore I beg such lazy paunches or presumptuous saints to be persuaded and believe for God's sake that they are verily, verily! not so learned or such great doctors as they imagine; and never to presume that they have finished learning this [the parts of the Catechism], or know it well enough in all points, even though they think that they know it ever so well. For though they should know and understand it perfectly (which, however, is impossible in this life), yet there are manifold benefits and fruits still to be obtained, if it be daily read and practised in thought and speech; namely, that the Holy Ghost is present in such reading and repetition and meditation, and bestows ever new and more light and devoutness, so that it is daily relished and appreciated better, as Christ promises, Matt. 18, 20: Where two or three are gathered together in My name, there am I in the midst of them.

Besides, it is an exceedingly effectual help against the devil, the world, and the flesh and all evil thoughts to be occupied with the Word of God, and to speak of it, and meditate upon it, so that the First Psalm declares those blessed who meditate upon the law of God day and night. Undoubtedly, you will not start a stronger incense or other fumigation against the devil than by being engaged upon God's commandments and words, and speaking, singing, or thinking of them. For this is indeed the true holy water and holy sign from which he flees, and by which he may be driven away.

Now, for this reason alone you ought gladly to read, speak, think and treat of these things if you had no other profit and fruit from them than that by doing so you can drive away the devil and evil thoughts. For he cannot hear or endure

God's Word; and God's Word is not like some other silly prattle, as that about Dietrich of Berne, etc., but as St. Paul says, Rom. 1, 16, the power of God. Yea, indeed, the power of God which gives the devil burning pain, and strengthens, comforts, and helps us beyond measure.

And what need is there of many words ? If I were to recount all the profit and fruit which God's Word produces, whence would I get enough paper and time? The devil is called the master of a thousand arts. But what shall we call God's Word, which drives away and brings to naught this master of a thousand arts with all his arts and power? It must indeed be the master of more than a hundred thousand arts. And shall we frivolously despise such power, profit, strength, and fruit — we, especially, who claim to be pastors and preachers? If so, we should not only have nothing given us to eat, but be driven out, being baited with dogs, and pelted with dung, because we not only need all this every day as we need our daily bread but must also daily use it against the daily and unabated attacks and lurking of the devil, the master of a thousand arts.

And if this were not sufficient to admonish us to read the Catechism daily, yet we should feel sufficiently constrained by the command of God alone, who solemnly enjoins in Deut. 6, 6 ff. that we should always meditate upon His precepts, sitting, walking, standing, Lying down, and rising, and have them before our eyes and in our hands as a constant mark and sign. Doubtless He did not so solemnly require and enjoin this without a purpose; but because He knows our danger and need, as well as the constant and furious assaults and temptations of devils, He wishes to warn, equip, and preserve us against them, as with a good armor against their fiery darts and with good medicine against their evil infection and suggestion.

Oh, what mad, senseless fools are we that, while we must ever live and dwell among such mighty enemies as the devils are, we nevertheless despise our weapons and defense, and are too lazy to look at or think of them!

And what else are such supercilious, presumptuous saints, who are unwilling to read and study the Catechism daily, doing than esteeming themselves much more learned than God Himself with all His saints, angels [patriarchs], prophets, apostles, and all Christians For inasmuch as God Himself is not ashamed to teach these things daily, as knowing nothing better to teach, and always keeps teaching the same thing, and does not take up anything new or different, and all the saints know nothing better or different to learn, and cannot finish learning this, are we not the finest of all fellows to imagine, if we have once read or heard it, that we know it all, and have no further need to read and learn, but can finish learning in one hour what God Himself cannot finish teaching, although He is engaged in teaching it from the beginning to the end of the world, and all prophets, together with all saints, have been occupied with learning it and have ever remained pupils, and must continue to be such ?

For it needs must be that whoever knows the Ten Commandments perfectly must know all the Scriptures, so that, in all affairs and cases, he can advise, help, comfort, judge, and decide both spiritual and temporal matters and is qualified to sit in judgment upon all doctrines, estates, spirits, laws, and whatever else is in the world. And what, indeed, is the entire Psalter but thoughts and exercises upon the First Commandment? Now I know of a truth that such lazy paunches and presumptuous spirits do not understand a single psalm, much less the entire Holy Scriptures; and yet they pretend to know and despise the Catechism, which is a compend and brief summary of all the Holy Scriptures.

Therefore I again implore all Christians, especially pastors and preachers, not to be doctors too soon, and imagine that they know everything (for imagination and cloth unshrunk [and false weights] fall far short of the measure), but that they daily exercise themselves well in these studies and constantly treat them; moreover, that they guard with all care and diligence against the poisonous infection of such security and vain imagination, but steadily keep on reading, teaching, learning, pondering, and meditating, and do not cease until they have made a test and are sure that they have taught the devil to death and have become more learned than God Himself and all His saints.

If they manifest such diligence, then I will promise them, and they shall also perceive, what fruit they will obtain, and what excellent men God will make of them, so that in due time they themselves will acknowledge that the longer and the more they study the Catechism, the less they know of it, and the more they find yet to learn; and then only, as hungry and thirsty ones, will they truly relish that which now they cannot endure because of great abundance and satiety. To this end may God grant His grace! Amen.

Short Preface of Dr. Martin Luther.

This sermon is designed and undertaken that it might be an instruction for children and the simple-minded. Hence of old it was called in Greek catechism, i.e., instruction for children, what every Christian must needs know, so that he who does not know this could not be numbered with the Christians nor be admitted to any Sacrament, just as a mechanic who does not understand the rules and customs of his trade is expelled and considered incapable. Therefore we must have the young learn the parts which belong to the Catechism or instruction for children well and fluently and diligently exercise themselves in them and keep them occupied with them.

Therefore it is the duty of every father of a family to question and examine his children and servants at least once a week and to ascertain what they know of it, or are learning and, if they do not know it, to keep them faithfully at it. For I well remember the time, indeed, even now it is a daily occurrence that one finds rude, old persons who knew nothing and still know nothing of these things, and who, nevertheless, go to Baptism and the Lord's Supper, and use everything belonging to Christians, notwithstanding that those who come to the Lord's Supper ought to know more and have a fuller understanding of all Christian doctrine than children and new scholars. However, for the common people we are satisfied with the three parts, which have remained in Christendom from of old, though little of it has been taught and treated correctly until both young and old who are called and wish to be Christians, are well trained in them and familiar with them. These are the following:

First.

The Ten Commandments of God.

1. Thou shalt have no other gods before Me.
2. Thou shalt not take the name of th Lord, thy God, in vain [for the Lord will not hold him guiltless that taketh His name in vain].
3. Thou shalt sanctify the holy-day. [Remember the Sabbath-day to keep it holy.]
4. Thou shalt honor thy father and mother [that thou mayest live long upon the earth].
5. Thou shlt not kill.
6. Thou shalt not commit adultery.
7. Thou shalt not steal.
8. Thou shalt not bear false witness against thy neighbor.
9. Thou shalt not covet thy neighbor's house.
10. Thou shalt not covet thy neighbor's wife, nor his man-servant, nor his

maidservant, nor his cattle [ox, nor his ass], nor anything that is his.

Secondly.

The Chief Articles of Our Faith.

1. I believe in God the Father Almighty, Maker of heaven and earth.
2. And in Jesus Christ, His only Son, our Lord; who was conceived by the Holy Ghost, born of the Virgin Mary; suffered under Pontius Pilate, was crucified, dead and buried; He descended into hell; the third day He rose again from the dead; He ascended into heaven, and sitteth on the right hand of God the Father Almighty; from thence He shall come to judge the quick and the dead.
3. I believe in the Holy Ghost, the holy Christian Church, the communion of saints, the forgiveness of sins, the resurrection of the body, and the life everlasting. Amen.

Thirdly.

The Prayer, or "Our Father," Which Christ Taught

Our Father who art in heaven.
1. Hallowed be Thy name.
2. Thy kingdom come.
3. Thy will be done on earth as it is in heaven.
4. Give us this day our daily bread.
5. And forgive us our trespasses as we forgive those who trespass against us.
6. And lead us not into temptation.
7. But deliver us from evil. [For Thine is the kingdom and the power and the glory, forever and ever.] Amen.

These are the most necessary parts which one should first learn to repeat word for word and which our children should be accustomed to recite daily when they arise in the morning when they sit down to their meals, and when they retire at night; and until they repeat them, they should be given neither food nor drink. Likewise every head of a household is obliged to do the same with respect to his domestics, ma-servants and maid-servants and not to keep them in his house if they do not know these things and are unwilling to learn them. For a person who is so rude and unruly as to be unwilling to learn these things is not to be tolerated, for in these three parts everything that we have in the Scriptures is comprehended in short, pain, and simple terms. For the holy Fathers or apostles (whoever they were) have thus embraced in a summary the doctrine, life, wisdom, and art of Christians, of which they speak and treat, and with which they are occupied.

Now, when these three arts are apprehended, it behooves a person also to know what to say concerning our Sacraments, which Christ Himself instituted, Baptism and the holy body and blood of Christ, namely, the text which Matthew [28, 19 ff.] and Mark [16, 15 f.] record at the close of their Gospels when Christ said farewell to His disciples and sent them forth.

Of Baptism.

Go ye and teach all nations, baptizing them in the name of the Father, and of the Son, and of the Holy Ghost. He that believeth and is baptized shall be saved; but he that believeth not shall be damned.

So much is sufficient for a simple person to know fro the Scriptures concerning Baptism. In like manner, also, concerning the other Sacrament in short, simple words, namely the text of St. Paul [1 Cor. 11, 23 f.].

Of the Sacrament

Our Lord Jesus Christ, the same night in which He was betrayed, took bread; and when He had given thanks, He brake it, and gave it to His disciples and said, Take, eat; this is My body, which is given for you: this do in remembrance of Me.

After the same manner also He took the cup, when He had supped, gave thanks, and gave it to them, saying, Drink ye all of it; this cup is the new testament in My blood, which is shed for you for the remission of sins: this do ye, as oft as ye drink it, in remembrance of Me.

Thus, ye would have, in all, five parts of the entire Christian doctrine which should be constantly treated and required [of children] and heard recited word for word. For you must not rely upon it that the young people will learn and retain these things from the sermon alone. When these parts have been well learned, you may, as a supplement and to fortify them. lay before them also some psalms or hymns, which have been composed on these parts, and thus lead the young into the Scriptures, and make daily progress therein.

However, it is not enough for them to comprehend and recite these parts according to the words only, but the young people should also be made to attend the preaching, espeially during the time which is devoted to the Catechism, that they may hear it explained and may learn to understand what every part contains, so as to be able to recite it as they have heard it, and, when asked, may give a correct answer, so that the preaching may not be without profit and fruit. For the reason why we exercise such diligence in preaching the Catechis so often is that it may be inculcated on our youth, not in a high and subtle manner, but briefly and with the greatest simplicity, so as to enter the mind readily and be fixed in the memory.

Therefore we shall now take up the abovementioned articles one by one and in the plainest manner possible say about them as much as is necessary.

Part First. The Ten Commandments.

The First Commandment.

Thou shalt have no other gods before Me.

That is: Thou shalt have [and worship] Me alone as thy God. What is the force of this, and how is it to be understood? What does it mean to have a god? or, what is God? Answer: A god means that from which we are to expect all good and to which we are to take refuge in all distress, so that to have a God is nothing else than to trust and believe Him from the [whole] heart; as I have often said that the confidence and faith of the heart alone make both God and an idol. If your faith and trust be right, then is your god also true; and, on the other hand, if your trust be false and wrong, then you have not the true God; for these two belong together faith and God. That now, I say, upon which you set your heart and put your trust is properly your god.

Therefore it is the intent of this commandment to require true faith and trust of the heart which settles upon the only true God and clings to Him alone. That is as much as to say: "See to it that you let Me alone be your God, and never seek another," i.e.: Whatever you lack of good things, expect it of Me, and look to Me for it, and whenever you suffer misfortune and distress, creep and cling to Me. I, yes, I, will give you enough and help you out of every need; only let not your heart cleave to or rest in any other.

This I must unfold somewhat more plainly, that it may be understood and perceived by ordinary examples of the contrary. Many a one thinks that he has God and everything in abundance when he has money and possessions; he trusts in them and boasts of them with such firmness and assurance as to care for no one. Lo, such a man also has a god, Mammon by name, i.e., money and possessions, on which he sets all his heart, and which is also the most common idol on earth. He who has money and possessions feels secure, and is joyful and undismayed as though he were sitting in the midst of Paradise. On the other hand, he who has none doubts and is despondent, as though he knew of no God. For very few are to be found who are of good cheer, and who neither mourn nor complain if they have not Mammon. This [care and desire for money] sticks and clings to our nature, even to the grave.

So, too, whoever trusts and boasts that he possesses great skill, prudence, power, favor friendship, and honor has also a god, but not this true and only God. This appears again when you notice how presumptuous, secure, and proud people are because of such possessions, and how despondent when they no longer exist or are withdrawn. Therefore I repeat that the chief explanation of this point is that to have a god is to have something in which the heart entirely trusts.

Besides, consider what in our blindness, we have hitherto been practising and doing under the Papacy. If any one had toothache, he fasted and honored St. Apollonia [[acerated his flesh by voluntary fasting to the honor of St. Apollonia]; if he was afraid of fire, he chose St. Lawrence as his helper in need; if he dreaded pestilence, he made a vow to St. Sebastian or Rochio, and a countless number of such abominations, where every one selected his own saint, worshiped him, and called for help to him in distress. Here belong those also, as, e.g., sorcerers and magicians, whose idolatry is most gross, and who make a covenant with the devil, in order that he may give them plenty of money or help them in love-affairs, preserve their cattle, restore to them lost possessions, etc. For all these place their heart and trust elsewhere than in the true God, look for nothing good to Him nor seek it from Him.

Thus you can easily understand what and how much this commandment requires, namely, that man's entire heart and all his confidence be placed in God alone, and in no one else. For to have God, you can easily perceive, is not to lay hold of Him with our hands or to put Him in a bag [as money], or to lock Him in a chest [as silver vessels]. But to apprehend Him means when the heart lays hold of Him and clings to Him. But to cling to Him with the heart is nothing else than to trust in Him entirey. For this reason He wishes to turn us away from everything else that exists outside of Him, and to draw us to Himself, namely, because He is the only eternal good. As though He would say: Whatever you have heretofore sought of the saints, or for whatever [things] you have trusted in Mammon or anything else, expect it all of Me, and regard Me as the one who will help you and pour out upon you richly all good things.

Lo, here you have the meaning of the true honor and worship of God, which pleases God, and which He commands under penalty of eternal wrath, namely, that the heart know no other comfort or confidence than in Him, and do not suffer itself to be torn from Him, but, for Him, risk and disregard everything upon earth. On the other hand, you can easily see and judge how the world practises only false worship and idolatry. For no people has ever been so reprobate as not to institute and observe some divine worship; every one has set up as his special god whatever he looked to for blessings, help, and comfort.

Thus, for example, the heathen who put their trust in power and dominion elevated Jupiter as the supreme god; the others, who were bent upon riches, happiness, or pleasure, and a life of ease, Hercules, Mercury, Venus or others; women with child, Diana or Lucina, and so on; thus every one made that his god to which his heart was inclined, so that even in the mind of the heathen to have a god means to trust and believe. But their error is this that their trust is false and wrong for it is not placed in the only God, besides whom there is truly no God in heaven or upon earth. Therefore the heathen really make their self-invented notions and dreams of God an idol, and put their trust in that which is altogether nothing. Thus it is with all idolatry; for it consists not merely in erecting an image and worshiping it, but rather in the heart, which stands gaping at something else, and seeks help and consolation from creatures saints, or devils, and neither cares for God, nor looks to Him for so much good as to believe that He is willing to help, neither believes that whatever good it experiences comes from God.

Besides, there is also a false worship and extreme idolatry, which we have hitherto practised, and is still prevalent in the world, upon which also all ecclesiastical orders are founded, and which concerns the conscience alone that seeks in its own works help, consolation, and salvation, presumes to wrest heaven from God, and reckons how many bequests it has made, how often it has fasted, celebrated Mass, etc. Upon such things it depends, and of them boasts, as though unwilling to receive anything from God as a gift, but desires itself to earn or merit it superabundantly, just as though He must serve us and were our debtor, and we His liege lords. What is this but reducing God to an idol, yea, [a fig image or] an apple-god, and elevating and regarding ourselves as God ? But this is slightly too subtle, and is not for young pupils.

But let this be said to the simple, that they may well note and remember the meaning of this commandment, namely, that we are to trust in God alone, and look to Him and expect from Him naught but good, as from one who gives us body, life, food, drink, nourishment, health, protection, peace, and all necessaries of both temporal and eternal things. He also preserves us from misfortune, and if any evil befall us, delivers and rescues us, so that it is God alone (as has been sufficiently said) from whom we receive all good, and by whom we are delivered from all evil. Hence also, I think, we Germans from ancient times call God (more elegantly and appropriately than any other language) by that name from the word good as being an eternal fountain which gushes forth abundantly nothing but what is good, and from which flows forth all that is and is called good.

For even though otherwise we experience much good from men, still whatever we receive by His command or arrangement is all received from God. For our parents, and all rulers, and every one besides with respect to his neighbor, have received from God the command that they should do us all manner of good, so that we receive these blessings not from them, but, through them, from God. For creatures are only the hands, channels, and means whereby God gives all things, as He gives to the mother breasts and milk to offer to her child, and corn and all manner of produce from the earth for nourishment, none of which blessings could be produced by any creature of itself.

Therefore no man should presume to take or give anything except as God has commanded, in order that it may be acknowledged as God's gift, and thanks may be rendered Him for it, as this commandment requires. On this account also these means of receiving good gifts through creatures are not to be rejected, neither should we in presumption seek other ways and means than God has commanded. For that would not be receiving from God, hut seeking of ourselves.

Let every one, then, see to it that he esteem this commandment great and high above all things, and do not regard it as a joke. Ask and examine your heart diligently, and you will find whether it cleaves to God alone or not. If you have a heart that can expect of Him nothing but what is good, especially in want and distress, and that, moreover renounces and forsakes everything that is not God, then you have the only true God. If on the contrary, it cleaves to anything else, of which it expects more good and help than of God, and does not take refuge in Him, but in adversity flees from Him, then you have an idol, another god.

In order that it may be seen that God will not have this commandment thrown to the winds, but will most strictly enforce it, He has attached to it first a terrible threat, and then a beautiful, comforting promise which is also to be urged and impressed upon young people, that they may take it to heart and retain it:

[Exposition of the Appendix to the First Commandment.]

For I am the Lord, thy God, strong and jealous, visiting the iniquity of the fathers upon the children unto the third and fourth generation of them that hate Me; and showing mercy unto thousands of them that love Me and keep My commandments.

Although these words relate to all the commandments (as we shall hereafter learn), yet they are joined to this chief commandment because it is of first importance that men have a right head; for where the head is right, the whole life must be right, and vice versa. Learn, therefore, from these words how angry God is with those who trust in anything but Him, and again, how good and gracious He is to those who trust and believe in Him alone with the whole heart; so that His anger does not cease until the fourth generation, while, on the other hand, His blessing and goodness extend to many thousands lest you live in such security and commit yourself to chance, as men of brutal heart, who think that it makes no great difference [how they live]. He is a God who will not leave it unavenged if men turn from Him, and will not cease to be angry until the fourth generation, even until they are utterly exterminated. Therefore He is to be feared, and not to be desisted.

He has also demonstrated this in all history, as the Scriptures abundantly show and daily experience still teaches. For from the beginning He has utterly extirpated all idolatry, and, on account of it, both heathen and Jews; even as at the present day He overthrows all false worship, so that all who remain therein must finally perish. Therefore, although proud, powerful, and rich worldlings [Sardanapaluses and Phalarides, who surpass even the Persians in wealth] are now to be found, who boast defiantly of their Mammon, with utter disregard whether God is angry at or smiles on them, and dare to withstand His wrath, yet they shall not succeed, but before they are aware,they shall be wrecked, with all in which they trusted; as all others have perished who have thought themselves more secure or powerful.

And just because of such hardened heads who imagine because God connives and allows them to rest in security, that He either is entirely ignorant or cares nothing about such matters, He must deal a smashing blow and punish them,,so that He cannot forget it unto children's children; so that every one may take note and see that this is no joke to Him. For they are those whom He means when He says: Who hate Me, i.e., those who persist in their defiance and pride; whatever is preached or said to them, they will not listen; when they are reproved, in order that they may learn to know themselves and amend before the punishment begins, they become mad and foolish so as to fairly merit wrath, as now we see daily in bishops and princes.

But terrible as are these threatenings, so much the more powerful is the consolation in the promise, that those who cling to God alone should be sure that He will show them mercy that is, show them pure goodness and blessing not only for themselves, but also to their children and children's children, even to the thousandth generation and beyond that. This ought certainly to move and impel us to risk our hearts in all confidence with God, if we wish all temporal and eternal good, since the Supreme Majesty makes such sublime offers and presents such cordial inducements and such rich promises.

Therefore let everyone seriously take this to heart, lest it be regarded as though a man had spoken it. For to you it is a question either of eternal blessing, happiness, and salvation, or of eternal wrath, misery, and woe. What more would you have or desire than that He so kindly promises to be yours with every blessing, and to protect and help you in all need?

But, alas! here is the failure, that the world believes nothing of this, nor regards it as God's Word, because it sees that those who trust in God and not in Mammon suffer care and want, and the devil opposes and resists them, that they have neither money, favor, nor honor, and, besides, can scarcely support life; while, on the other hand, those who serve Mammon have power, favor, honor, possessions, and every comfort in the eyes of the world. For this reason, these words must be grasped as being directed against such appearances; and we must consider that they do not lie or deceive, but must come true.

Reflect for yourself or make inquiry and tell me: Those who have employed all their care and diligence to accumulate great possessions and wealth, what have they finally attained? You will find that they have wasted their toil and labor, or even though they have amassed great treasures, they have been dispersed and scattered, so that the themselves have never found happiness in their wealth, and afterwards never reached the third generation.

Instances of this you will find a plenty in all histories, also in the memory of aged and experienced people. Only observe and ponder them.

Saul was a great king, chosen of God and a godly man; but when he was established on his throne, and let his heart decline from God, and put his trust in his crown and power, he had to perish with all that he had, so that none even of his children remained.

David, on the other hand, was a poor, despised man, hunted down and chased, so that he nowhere felt secure of his life; yet he had to remain in spite of Saul, and become king. For these words had to abide and come true, since God cannot lie or deceive. Only let not the devil and the world deceive you with their show, which indeed remains for a time, but finally is nothing.

Let us, then, learn well the First Commandment, that we may see how God will tolerate no presumption nor any trust in any other object, and how He requires nothing higher of us than confidence from the heart for everything good, so that we may proceed right and straightforward and use all the blessings which God gives no farther than as a shoemaker uses his needle, awl, and thread for work, and then lays them aside, or as a traveler uses an inn, and food, and his bed only for temporal necessity, each one in his station, according to God's order, and without allowing any of these things to be our food or idol. Let this suffice with respect to the First Commandment, which we have had to explain at length, since it is of chief importance, because, as before said, where the heart is rightly disposed toward God and this commandment is observed, all the others follow.

The Second Commandment.

Thou shalt not take the name of the Lord, thy God, in vain.

As the First Commandment has instructed the heart and taught [the basis of] faith, so this commandment leads us forth and directs the mouth and tongue to God. For the first objects that spring from the heart and manifest themselves are words. Now, as I have taught above how to answer the question, what it is to have a god, so you must learn to comprehend simply the meaning of this and all the commandments, and to apply it to yourself.

If, then, it be asked: How do you understand the Second Commandment, or what is meant by taking in vain, or misusing God's name? answer briefly thus: It is misusing God's name when we call upon the Lord God no matter in what way, for purposes of falsehood or wrong of any kind. Therefore this commandment enjoins this much, that God's name must not be appealed to falsely, or taken upon the lips while the heart knows well enough, or should know, differently; as among those who take oaths in court, where one side lies against the other. For God's name cannot be misused worse than for the support of falsehood and deceit. Let4this remain the exact German and simplest meaning of this commandment.

From this every one can readily infer when and in how many ways God's name is misused, although it is impossible to enumerate all its misuses. Yet, to tell it in a few words, all misuse of the divine name occurs, first, in worldly business and in matters which concern money, possessions, honor, whether it be publicly in court, in the market, or wherever else men make false oaths in God's name, or pledge their souls in any matter. And this is especially prevalent in marriage affairs where two go and secretly betroth themselves to one another, and afterward abjure [their plighted troth].

But. the greatest abuse occurs in spiritual matters, which pertain to the conscience, when false preachers rise up and offer their Lying vanities as God's Word.

Behold, all this is decking one's self out with God's name, or making a pretty show, or claiming to be right, whether it occur in gross, worldly business or in sublime, subtile matters of faith and doctrine. And among liars belong also blasphemers, not alone the very gross, well known to every one, who disgrace God's name without fear (these are not for us, but for the hangman to discipline); but also those who publicly traduce the truth and God's Word and consign it to the devil. Of this there is no need now to speakfurther.

Here, then, let us learn and take to heart the great importance of this commandment, that with all diligence we may guard against and dread every misuse of the holy name, as the greatest sin that can be outwardly committed. For to lie and deceive is in itself a great sin, but is greatly aggravated when we attempt to justify it, and seek to confirm it by invoking the name of God and usiig it as a cloak for shame, so that from a single lie a double lie, nay, manifold lies, result.

For this reason, too, God has added a solemn threat to this commandment, to wit: For the Lord will not hold him guiltless that taketh His name in van. That is: It shall not be condoned to any one nor pass unpunished. For as little as He will leave it unavenged if any one turn his heart from Him, as little will He suffer His name to be employed for dressing up a lie. Now alas! it is a common calamity in all the word that there are as few who are not using the name of God for purposes of Lying and all wickedness as there are those who with their heart trust alone in God.

For by nature we all have within us this beautiful virtue, to wit, that whoever has committed a wrong would like to cover up and adorn his disgrace, so that no one may see it or know it; and no one is so bold$as to boast to all the world of the wickedness he has perpetrated, all wish to act by stealth and without any one being aware of what thy do. Then, if any one be arraigned, the name of God is dragged into the affair and must make the villainy look like godliness, and the shame like honor. This is the common course of the world, hich, like a great deluge, has flooded all lands. Hence we have also as our reward what we seek and deserve: pestilences wars, famines, conflagrations, floods, wayward wives, children, servants, and all sorts of defilement. Whence else should so much misery come? It is still a great mercy that the earth bears and supports us.

Therefore, above all things, our young people should have this commandment earnestly enforced upon them, and they should be trined to hold this and the First Commandment in high regard; and whenever they transgress, we must at once be after them with the rod and hold the commandment before them, andconstantly inculcate it, so as to bring them up not only with punishment, but also in the reverence and fear of God.

Thus you now understand what. it is to take God's name in vain, that is (to recapitulate briefly), eiher simply for purposes of falsehood, and to allege God's name for something that is not so, or to curse, swear, conjure, and, in short, to practise whhtever wickedness one may.

Besides this you must also know how to use the name [of God] aright. For when saying: Thou shalt not take the name of the Lord thy God, in vain, He gives us to understand at the same time that it is to be used properly. For it has been revealed and given to us for the very purpose that it may be of constant use and profit. Hence it is a natural inference, since using the holy name for falsehood or wickedness is here forbidden, that we are, on the other hand, commanded to employ it for truth and for all good, as when one swears truly where there is need and it is demanded. So also when there is right teaching, and when the name is invoked in trouble or praised and thanked in prosperity etc.; all of which is comprehended summarily and commanded in the passage Ps. 50, 15: Call upon Me in the days of trouble; I will deliver thee, and thou shalt glorify Me. For all this is bringing 't into the service of truth, and using it in a blessed way, and thus His name is hallowed, as we pray in the Lord's Prayer.

Thus you have the sum of the entire commandment explained. And with this understanding the question with which many teachers have troubled themselves has been easily solved, to wit, why swearing is prohibited in the Gospel, and yet Christ, St. Paul, and other saints often swore. The explanation is briefly this: We are not to swear in support of evil, that is, of falsehood, and where there is no need or use; but for the support of good and the advantage of our neighbor we should swear. For it is a truly good work, by which God is praised, truth and right are established, falsehood is refuted, peace is made among men, obedience is rendered, and quarrels are settled. For in this way God Himself interposes and separates between right and wrong, good and evil. If one part swears falsely, he has his sentence that he shall not escape punishment, ad though it be deferred a long time, he shall not succeed; that all that he may gain thereby will slip out of his hands, and he will never enjoy it; as I have seen in the case of many who perjured themselves in their marriage-vows, that they have never had a happy hour or a healthful day, and thus perished miserably in body, soul, and possessions.

Therefore I advise and exhort as before that by means of warning and threatening, restraint and punishment, the children be trained betimes to shun falsehood, and especially to avoid the use oo God's ame in its support. For where they are allowed to do as they please, no good will result, aa is even now evident that the world is worse than it has ever been and that there is no government, no obedience, no fidelity, no faith, but only daring, unbridled men, whom no teaching or reproof helps; all of which is God's wrath and punishment for such wanton contempt of this commandment.

On the other hand, they should be constantly urged and incited to honor God's name, and to have it always upon their lips in everything that may happen to them or come to their notice: For that is the true honor of His Name, to look to it and implore it for all consolation, so that (as we have heard above) first the heart by faith gives God the honor due Him, and afterwards the lips by confession.

This is also a blessed and useful habit and very effectual against the devil, who is ever about us, and lies in wait to bring us into sin and shame, calamity and trouble, but who is very loath to hear God's name, and cannot remain long where it is uttered and called upon from the heart. And, indeed, many a terrible and shocking calamity would befall us if, by our calling upon His name, God did not preserve us. I have myself tried it, and learned by experience that often sudden great calamity was immediately averted and removed during such invocation. To vex the devil, I say, we should always have this holy name in oor mouth, so that he may not be able to injure us as he wishes.

For this end it is also of service that we form the habit of daily commending ourselves to God, with soul and body, wife, children, servants, and all that we have, against every need that may occur; whence also the blessing and thanksgiving at meals, and other prayers, morning and evening, have originated and remain in use. Likewise the practises of children to cross themselves when anything monstrous or terrible is seen or heard, and to exclaim: "Lord God, protect us!" "Help, dear Lord Jesus!" etc. Thus, too, if any one meets with unexpected good fortune, however trivial, that he say: "God be praised and thanked; this God has bestowed on me!" etc., as formerly the children were accustomed to fast and pray to St. Nicholas and other saints. This would be more pleasing and acceptable to God than all monasticism and Carthusian sanctity.

Behold, thus we might train our youth in a childlike way and playfully in the fear and honor of God, so that the First and Second Commandments might be well observed and in constant practise. Then some good might take root, spring up and bear fruit, and men grow up whom an entire land might relish and enjoy. Moreover, this would be the true way to bring Up children well as long as they can become trained with kinnness and delight. For what must be enforced with rods and blows only will not develop into a good breed and at best they will remain godly under such treatment no longer than while the rod is upon their back.

But this [manner of training] so spreads its roots in the heart that they fear

God more than rods and clubs. This I say with such simplicity for the sake of the young, that it may penetrate their minds. For since we are preaching to children, we must also prattle with them. Thus we have prevented the abuse and have taught the right use of the divine name, which should consist not only in words, but also in practises and life, so that we may know that God is well pleased with this and will as richly reward it as He will terribly punish the abuse.

The Third Commandment.

Thou shalt sanctify the holy day.
[Remember the Sabbath day to keep it holy.]

The word holy day (Feiertag) is rendered from the Hebrew word sabbath which properly signifies to rest, that is, to abstain from labor. Hence we are accustomed to say, Feierbend machen [that is, to cease working], or heiligen Abend geben [sanctify the Sabbath]. Now, in the Old Testament, God separated the seventh day, and appointed it for rest, and commanded that it should be regarded as holy above all others. As regards this external observance, this commandment was given to the Jews alone, that they should abstain from toilsome work, and rest, so that both man and beast might recuperate, and not be weakened by unremitting labor. Although they afterwards restricted this too closely, and grossly abused it, so that they traduced and could not endure in Christ those works which they themselves were accustomed to do on that day, as we read in the Gospel just as though the commandment were fulfilled by doing no external [manual] work whatever, which, however, was not the meaning, but, as we shall hear, that they sanctify the holy day or day of rest.

This commandment, therefore, according to its gross sense, does not concern us Christians; for it is altogether an external matter, like other ordinances of the Old Testament, which were attached to particular customs, persons, times, and places, and now have been made free through Christ.

But to grasp a Christian meaning for the simple as to what God requires in this commandment, note that we keep holy days not for the sake of intelligent and learned Christians (for they have no need of it [holy days]), but first of all for bodily causes and necessities, which nature teaches and requires; for the common people, man-servants and maid-servants, who have been attending to their work and trade the whole week, that for a day they may retire in order to rest and be refreshed.

Secondly, and most especially, that on such day of rest (since we can get no other opportunity) freedom and time be taken to attend divine service, so that we come together to hear and treat of God's and then to praise God, to sing and pray.

However, this, I say, is not so restricted to any time, as with the Jews, that it must be just on this or that day; for in itself no one day is better than another; but this should indeed be done daily; however, since the masses cannot give such attendance, there must be at least one day in the week set apart. But since from of old Sunday [the Lord's Day] has been appointed for this purpose, we also should continue the same, in order that everything be done in harmonious order, and no one create disorder by unnecessary innovation.

Therefore this is the simple meaning of the commandment: since holidays are observed anyhow, such observance should be devoted to hearing God's Word, so that the special function of this day should be the ministry of the Word for the young and the mass of poor people, yet that the resting be not so strictly interpreted as to forbid any other incidental work that cannot be avoided.

Accordingly, when asked, What is meant by the commandment: Thou shalt sanctify the holy day? answer: To sanctify the holy day is the same as to keep it holy. But what is meant by keeping it holy? Nothing else than to be occupied in holy words, works, and life. For the day needs no sanctification for itself; for in itself it has been created holy [from the beginning of the creation it was sanctified by its Creator]. But God desires it to be holy to you. Therefore it becomes holy or unholy on your account, according as you are occupied on the same with things that are holy or unholy.

How, then, does such sanctification take place? Not in this manner, that [with folded hands] we sit behind the stove and do no rough [external] work, or deck ourselves with a wreath and put on our best clothes, but (as has been said) that we occupy ourselves with God's Word, and exercise ourselves therein.

And, indeed, we Christians ought always to keep such a holy day, and be occupied with nothing but holy things, i.e., daily be engaged upon God's Word, and carry it in our hearts and upon our lips. But (as has been said) since we do not at all times have leisure, we must devote several hours a week for the sake of the young, or at least a day for the sake of the entire multitude, to being concerned about this alone, and especially urge the Ten Commandments, the Creed, and the Lord's Prayer, and thus direct our whole life and being according to God's Word. At whatever time, then, this is being observed and practised, there a true holy day is being kept; otherwise it shall not be called a Christians' holy day. For, indeed, non-Christians can also cease from work and be idle, just as the entire swarm of our ecclesiastics, who stand daily in the churches, singing, and ringing bells but keeping no holy day holy, because they neither preach nor practises God's Word, but teach and live contrary to it.

For the Word of God is the sanctuary above all sanctuaries, yea, the only one which we Christians know and have. For though we had the bones of all the saints or all holy and consecrated garments upon a heap, still that would help us nothing; for all that is a dead thing which can sanctify nobody. But God's Word is the treasure which sanctifies everything, and by which even all the saints themselves were sanctified. At whatever hour then, God's Word is taught, preached, heard, read or meditated upon, there the person, day, and work are sanctified thereby, not because of the external work, but because of the Word which makes saints of us all. Therefore I constantly say that all our life and work must be ordered according to God's Word, if it is to be God-pleasing or holy. Where this is done, this commandment is in force and being fulfilled.

On the contrary, any observance or work that is practised without God's Word is unholy before God, no matter how brilliantly it may shine! even though it be covered with relics, such as the fictitious spiritual orders which know nothing of God's Word and seek holiness in their own works.

Note, therefore, that the force and power of this commandment lies not in the resting but in the sanctifying so that to this day belongs a special holy exercise. For other works and occupations are not properly called holy exercises, unless the man himself be first holy. But here a work is to be done by which man is himself made holy, which is done (as we have heard) alone through God's Word. For this, then, fixed places, times, persons, and the entire external order of worship have been created and appointed, so that it may be publicly in operation.

Since, therefore, so much depends upon God's Word that without it no holy day can be sanctified, we must know that God insists upon a strict observance of this commandment, and will punish all who despise His Word and are not willing to hear and learn it, especially at the time appointed for the purpose.

Therefore not only those sin against this commandment who grossly misuse and desecrate the holy day, as those who on account of their greed or frivolity neglect to hear God's Word or lie in taverns and are dead drunk like swine; but also that other crowd, who listen to God's Word as to any other trifle, and only from custom come to preaching, and go away again, and at the end of the year know as little of it as at the beginning. For hitherto the opinion prevailed that you had properly hallowed Sunday when you had heard a mass or the Gospel read; but no one cared for God's Word, as also no one taught it. Now, while we have God's Word we nevertheless do not correct the abuse; we suffer ourselves to be preached to and admonished, but we listen without seriousness and care.

Know, therefore, that you must be concerned not only about hearing, but also about learning and retaining it in memory, and do not think that it is optional with you or of no great importance, but that it is God's commandment, who will require of you how you have heard, learned, and honored His Word.

Likewise those fastidious spirits are to be reproved who, when they have heard a sermon or two, find it tedious and dull, thinking that they know all that well enough, and need no more instruction. For just that is the sin which has been hitherto reckoned among mortal sins, and is called _achedia_, i.e., torpor or satiety, a malignant, dangerous plague with which the devil bewitches and deceives the hearts of many, that he may surprise us and secretly withdraw God's Word from us.

For let me tell you this, even though you know it perfectly and be already master in all things, still you are daily in the dominion of the devil, who ceases neither day nor night to steal unawares upon you, to kindle in your heart unbelief and wicked thoughts against the foregoing and all the commandments. Therefore you must always have God's Word in your heart, upon your lips, and in your ears. But where the heart is idle, and the Word does not sound, he breaks in and has done the damage before we are aware. On the other hand, such is the efficacy of the Word, whenever it is seriously contemplated heard, and used, that it is bound never to be without fruit, but always awakens new understanding, pleasure, and devoutness, and produces a pure heart and pure thoughts. For these words are not inoperative or dead, but creative, living words. And even though no other interest or necessity impel us, yet this ought to urge every one thereunto, because thereby the devil is put to flight and driven away, and, besides, this commandment is fulfilled, and [this exercise in the Word] is more pleasing to God than any work of hypocrisy, however brilliant.

The Fourth Commandment.

Thus far we have learned the first three commandments, which relate to God. First that with our whole heart we trust in Him, and fear and love Him throughout all our life. Secondly, that we do not misuse His holy name in the support of falsehood or any bad work, but employ it to the praise of God and the profit and salvation of our neighbor and ourselves. Thirdly, that on holidays and when at rest we diligently treat and urge God's Word, so that all our actions and our entire life be ordered according to it. Now follow the other seven, which relate to our neighbor among which the first and greatest is:

Thou shalt honor thy father and thy mother.

To this estate of fatherhood and motherhood God has given the special distinction above all estates that are beneath it that He not simply commands us to love our parents, but to honor them. For with respect to brothers, sisters, and our neighbors in general He commands nothing higher than that we love them, so that He separates and distinguishes father and mother above all other persons upon earth, and places them at His side. For it is a far higher thing to honor than to love one, inasmuch as it comprehends not only love, but also modesty, humility, and deference as to a majesty there hidden, and requires not only that they be addressed kindly and with reverence, but, most of all that both in heart and with the body we so act as to show that we esteem them very highly, and that, next to God, we regard them as the very highest. For one whom we are to honor from the heart we must truly regard as high and great.

We must, therefore impress it upon the young that they should regard their parents as in God's stead, and remember that however lowly, poor, frail, and queer they may be, nevertheless they are father and mother given them by God. They are not to be deprived of their honor because of their conduct or their failings. Therefore we are not to regard their persons, how they may be, but the will of God who has thus created and ordained. In other respects we are, indeed, all alike in the eyes of God; but among us there must necessarily be such inequality and ordered difference, and therefore God commands it to be observed, that you obey me as your father, and that I have the supremacy.

Learn, therefore, first, what is the honor towards parents required by this commandment to wit, that they be held in distinction and esteem above all things, as the most precious treasure on earth. Furthermore, that also in our words we observe modesty toward them, do not accost them roughly, haughtily, and defiantly, but yield to them and be silent even though they go too far. Thirdly, that we show them such honor also by works, that is, with our body and possessions, that we serve them, help them, and provide for them when they are old, sick, infirm, or poor, and all that not only gladly, but with humility and reverence, as doing it before God. For he who knows how to regard them in his heart will not allow them to suffer want or hunger, but will place them above him and at his side, and will share with them whatever he has and possesses.

Secondly, notice how great, good, and holy a work is here assigned children, which is alas! utterly neglected and disregarded, and no one perceives that God has commanded it or that it is a holy, divine Word and doctrine. For if it had been regarded as such, every one could have inferred that they must be holy men who live according to these words. Thus there would have been no need of inventing monasticism nor spiritual orders, but every child would have abided by this commandment, and could have directed his conscience to God and said: "If I am to do good and holy works, I know of none better than to render all honor and obedience to my parents, because God has Himself commanded it. For what God commands must be much and far nobler than everything that we may devise ourselves, and since there is no higher or better teacher to be found than God, there can be no better doctrine, indeed, than He gives forth. Now, He teaches fully what we should do if we wish to perform truly good works, and by commanding them, He shows that they please Him. If, then, it is God who commands this, and who knows not how to appoint anything better, I will never improve upon it."

Behold, in this manner we would have had a godly child properly taught, reared in true blessedness, and kept at home in obedience to his parents and in their service, so that men should have had blessing and joy from the spectacle. However, God's commandment was not permitted to be thus [with such care and diligence] commended, but had to be neglected and trampled under foot, so that a child could not lay it to heart, and meanwhile gaped [like a panting wolf] at the devices which we set up, without once [consulting or] giving reverence to

God.

Let us, therefore, learn at last, for God's sake, that, placing all other things out of sight, our youths look first to this commandment, if they wish to serve God with truly good works, that they do what is pleasing to their fathers and mothers, or to those to whom they may be subject in their stead. For every child that knows and does this has, in the first place, this great consolation in his heart that he can joyfully say and boast (in spite of and against all who are occupied with works of their own choice): "Behold, this work is well pleasing to my God in heaven that I know for certain." Let them all come together with their many great, distressing, and difficult works and make their boast, we will see whether they can show one that is greater and nobler than obedience to father and mother, to whom God has appointed and commanded obedience next to His own majesty; so that if God's Word and will are in force and being accomplished nothing shall be esteemed higher than the will and word of parents; yet so that it, too, is subordinated to obedience toward God and is not opposed to the preceding commandments.

Therefore you should be heartily glad and thank God that He has chosen you and made you worthy to do a work so precious and pleasing to Him. Only see that, although it be regarded as the most humble and despised you esteem it great and precious, not on account of our worthiness, but because it is comprehended in, and controlled by, the jewel and sanctuary, namely, the Word and commandment of God. Oh, what a high price would all; Carthusians, monks, and nuns pay, if in all their religious doings they could bring into God's presence a single work done by virtue of His commandment, and be able before His face to say with joyful heart: "Now I know that this work is well pleasing to Thee." Where will these poor wretched persons hide when in the sight of God and all the world they shall blush with shame before a young child who has lived according to this commandment, and shall have to confess that with their whole life they are not worthy to give it a drink of water? And it serves them right for their devilish perversion in treading God's commandment under foot that they must vainly torment themselves with works of their own device, and, in addition, have scorn and loss for their reward.

Should not the heart, then, leap and melt for joy when going to work and doing what is commanded, saying: Lo, this is better than all holiness of the Carthusians, even though they kill themselves fasting and praying upon their knees without ceasing? For here you have a sure text and a divine testimony that He has enjoined this, but concerning the other He did not command a word. But this is the plight and miserable blindness of the world that no one believes these things; to such an extent the devil has deceived us with false holiness and the glamour of our own works.

Therefore I would be very glad (I say it again) if men would open their eyes and ears and take this to heart, lest some time we may again be led astray from the pure Word of God to the lying vanities of the devil. Then, too, all would be well; for parents would have more joy, love, friendship, and concord in their houses; thus the children could captivate their parents' hearts. On the other hand, when they are obstinate, and will not do what they ought until a rod is laid upon their back, they anger both God and their parents, whereby they deprive themselves of this treasure and joy of conscience and lay up for themselves only misfortune. Therefore, as every one complains, the course of the world now is such that both young and old are altogether dissolute and beyond control, have no reverence nor sense of honor, do nothing except as they are driven to it by blows, and perpetrate what wrong and detraction they can behind each other's back; therefore God also punishes them, that they sink into all kinds of filth and misery. As a rule, the parents, too, are themselves stupid and ignorant; one fool trains [teaches] another, and as they have lived, so live their children after them.

This, now, I say should be the first and most important consideration to urge us to the observance of this commandment; on which account, even if we had no father and mother we ought to wish that God would set up wood and stone before Us, whom we might call father and mother. How much more, since He has given us living parents, should we rejoice to show them honor and obedience, because we know it is so highly pleasing to the Divine Majesty and to all angels, and vexes all devils, and is, besides, the highest work which we can do, after the sublime divine worship comprehended in the previous commandments, so that giving of alms and every other good work toward our neighbor are not equal to this. For God has assigned this estate the highest place, yea, has set it up in His own stead, upon earth. This will and pleasure of God ought to be a sufficient reason and incentive to us to do what we can with good will and pleasure.

Besides this, it is our duty before the world to be grateful for benefits and every good which we have of our parents. But here again the devil rules in the world, so that the children forget their parents, as we all forget God, and no one considers how God nourishes, protects, and defends us, and bestows so much good on body and soul; especially when an evil hour comes we are angry and grumble with impatience and all the good which we have received throughout our life is wiped out [from our memory]. Just so we do also with our parents, and there is no child that understands and considers this [what the parents have endured while nourishing and fostering him], except the Holy Ghost grant him this grace.

God knows very well this perverseness of the world; therefore He admonishes and urges by commandments that every one consider what his parents have done for him and he will find that he has from them body and life, moreover, that he has been fed and reared when otherwise he would have perished a hundred times in his own filth. Therefore it is a true and good saying of old and wise men: Deo, parentibus et magistris non potest satis gratiae rependi, that is, To God, to parents, and to teachers we can never render sufficient gratitude and compensation. He that regards and considers this will indeed without compulsion do all honor to his parents, and bear them up on his hands as those through whom God has done him all good.

Over and above all this, another great reason that should incite us the more [to obedience to this commandment] is that God attaches to this commandment a temporal promise and says: That thou mayest live long upon the land which the Lord, thy God, giveth thee.

Here you can see yourself how much God is in earnest in respect to this commandment, inasmuch as He not only declares that it is well pleasing to Him, and that He has joy and delight therein; but also that it shall be for our prosperity and promote our highest good; so that we may have a pleasant and agreeable life, furnished with every good thing. Therefore also St. Paul greatly emphasizes the same and rejoices in it when he says, Eph. 6, 2. 3: This is the first commandment with promise: That it may be well with thee, and thou mayest live long on the earth. For although the rest also have their promises contained in them, yet in none is it so plainly and explicitly stated.

Here, then, you have the fruit and the reward, that whoever observes this commandment shall have happy days, fortune, and prosperity; and on the other hand, the punishment, that whoever is disobedient shall the sooner perish, and never enjoy life. For to have long life in the sense of the Scriptures is not only to become old, but to have everything which belongs to long life, such as health, wife, and children, livelihood, peace, good government, etc., without which this life can neither be enjoyed in cheerfulness nor long endure. If, therefore, you will not obey father and mother and submit to their discipline, then obey the hangman; if you will not obey him, then submit to the skeleton-man, i.e., death [death the all-subduer, the teacher of wicked children]. For on this God insists peremptorily: Either if you obey Him rendering love and service, He will reward you abundantly with all good, or if you offend Him, He will send upon you both death and the hangman.

Whence come so many knaves that must daily be hanged, beheaded, broken upon the wheel, but from disobedience [to parents], because they will not submit to discipline in kindness, so that, by the punishment of God, they bring it about that we behold their misfortune and grief? For it seldom happens that such perverse people die a natural or timely death.

But the godly and obedient have this blessing, that they live long in pleasant quietness and see their children's children (as said above) to the third and fourth generation.

Thus experience also teaches, that where there are honorable, old families who fare well and have many children, they owe their origin to the fact, to be sure, that some of them were brought up well and were regardful of their parents. On the other hand, it is written of the wicked, Ps. 109,13: Let his posterity be cut off; and in the generation following let their name be blotted out. Therefore heed well how great a thing in God's sight obedience is since He so highly esteems it, is so highly pleased with it, and rewards it so richly, and besides enforces punishment so rigorously on those who act contrariwise.

All this I say that it may be well impressed upon the young. For no one believes how necessary this commandment is, although it has not been esteemed and taught hitherto under the papacy. These are simple and easy words, and everybody thinks he knew them a fore; therefore men pass them lightly by, are gaping after other matters, and do not see and believe that God is so greatly offended if they be disregarded, nor that one does a work so well pleasing and precious if he follows them.

In this commandment belongs a further statement regarding all kinds of obedience to persons in authority who have to command and to govern. For all authority flows and is propagated from the authority of parents. For where a father is unable alone to educate his [rebellious and irritable] child, he employs a schoolmaster to instruct him; if he be too weak, he enlists the aid of his friends and neighbors; if he departs this life, he delegates and confers his authority and government upon others who are appointed for the purpose. Likewise, he must have domestics, man-servants and maid-servants, under himself for the management of the household, so that all whom we call masters are in the place of parents and must derive their power and authority to govern from them. Hence also they are all called fathers in the Scriptures, as those who in their government perform the functions of a father, and should have a paternal heart toward their subordinates. As also from antiquity the Romans and other nations called the masters and mistresses of the household patres-et matresfamiliae that is, housefathers and housemothers. So also they called their national rulers and overlords patres patriae, that is fathers of the entire country, for a great shame to us who would be Christians that we do not likewise call them so, or, at least do not esteem and honor them as such.

Now, what a child owes to father and mother, the same owe all who are embraced in the household. Therefore man-servants and maid-servants should be careful not only to be obedient to their masters and mistresses but also to honor them as their own fathers and mothers, and to do everything which they know is expected of them, not from compulsion and with reluctance, but with pleasure and joy for the cause just mentioned, namely that it is God's command and is pleasing to Him above all other works. Therefore they ought rather to pay wages in addition and be glad that they may obtain masters and mistresses to have such joyful consciences and to know how they may do truly golden works; a matter which has hitherto been neglected and despised, when, instead, everybody ran in the devil's name, into convents or to pilgrimages and indulgences, with loss [of time and money] and with an evil conscience.

If this truth, then, could be impressed upon the poor people, a servant-girl would leap and praise and thank God; and with her tidy work for which she receives support and wages she would acquire such a treasure as all that are esteemed the greatest saints have not obtained. Is it not an excellent boast to know and say that, if you perform your daily domestic task, this is better than all the sanctity and ascetic life of monks? And you have the promise, in addition, that you shall prosper in all good and fare well. How can you lead a more blessed or holier life as far as your works are concerned? For in the sight of God faith is what really renders a person holy, and alone serves Him, but the works are for the service of man. There you have everything good, protection and defense in the Lord, a joyful conscience and a gracious God besides, who will reward you a hundredfold, so that you are even a nobleman if you be only pious and obedient. But if not, you have, in the first place, nothing but the wrath and displeasure of God, no peace of heart, and afterwards all manner of plagues and misfortunes.

Whoever will not be influenced by this and inclined to godliness we hand over to the hangman and to the skeleton-man. Therefore let every one who allows himself to be advised remember that God is not making sport, and know that it is God who speaks with you and demands obedience. If you obey Him, you are His dear child; but if you despise to do it, then take shame, misery, and grief for your reward.

The same also is to be said of obedience to civil government, which (as we have said) is all embraced in the estate of fatherhood and extends farthest of all relations. For here the father is not one of a single family, but of as many people as he has tenants, citizens, or subjects. For through them, as through our parents, God gives to us food, house and home, protection and security. Therefore since they bear such name and title with all honor as their highest dignity, it is our duty to honor them and to esteem them great as the dearest treasure and the most precious jewel upon earth.

He, now, who is obedient here, is willing and ready to serve, and cheerfully does all that pertains to honor, knows that he is pleasing God and that he will receive joy and happiness for his reward. If he will not do it in love, but despises and resists [authority] or rebels, let him also know, on the other hand, that he shall have no favor nor blessing, and where he thinks to gain a florin thereby, he will elsewhere lose ten times as much, or become a victim to the hangman, perish by war, pestilence, and famine, or experience no good in his children, and be obliged to suffer injury, injustice, and violence at the hands of his servants, neighbors, or strangers and tyrants; so that what we seek and deserve is paid back and comes home to us.

If we would ever suffer ourselves to be persuaded that such works are pleasing to God and have so rich a reward, we would be established in altogether abundant possessions and have what our heart desires. But because the word and command of God are so lightly esteemed, as though some babbler had spoken it, let us see whether you are the man to oppose Him. How difficult, do you think, it will be for Him to recompense you! Therefore you would certainly live much better with the divine favor, peace, and happiness than with His displeasure and misfortune. Why, think you, is the world now so full of unfaithfulness, disgrace, calamity, and murder, but because every one desires to be his own master and free from the emperor, to care nothing for any one, and do what pleases him? Therefore God punishes one knave by another, so that, when you defraud and despise your master, another comes and deals in like manner with you, yea, in your household you must suffer ten times more from wife, children, or servants.

Indeed, we feel our misfortune, we murmur and complain of unfaithfulness, violence, and injustice, but will not see that we ourselves are knaves who have fully deserved this punishment, and yet are not thereby reformed. We will have no favor and happiness, therefore it is but fair that we have nothing but misfortune without mercy. There must still be somewhere upon earth some godly people because God continues to grant us so much good! On our own account we should not have a farthing in the house nor a straw in the field. All this I have been obliged to urge with so many words, in hope that some one may take it to heart, that we may be relieved of the blindness and misery in which we are steeped so deeply, and may truly understand the Word and will of God, and earnestly accept it. For thence we would learn how we could have joy, happiness, and salvation enough, both temporal and eternal.

Thus we have two kinds of fathers presented in this commandment, fathers in blood and fathers in office, or those to whom belongs the care of the family, and those to whom belongs the care of the country. Besides these there are yet spiritual fathers; not like those in the Papacy, who have indeed had themselves called thus, but have performed no function of the paternal office. For those only are called spiritual fathers who govern and guide us by the Word of God; as St. Paul boasts his fatherhood 1 Cor. 4, 15, where he says: In Christ Jesus I hove begotten you through the Gospel. Now, since they are fathers they are entitled to their honor, even above all others. But here it is bestowed least; for the way which the world knows for honoring them is to drive them out of the country and to grudge them a piece of bread and, in short, they must be (as says St. Paul 1 Cor. 4, 13) as the filth of the world and everybody's refuse and footrag.

Yet there is need that this also be urged upon the populace, that those who would be Christians are under obligation in the sight of God to esteem them worthy of double honor who minister to their souls, that they deal well with them and provide for them. For that, God is willing to add to you sufficient blessing and will not let you come to want. But in this matter every one refuses and resists, and all are afraid that they will perish from bodily want, and cannot now support one respectable preacher, where formerly they filled ten fat paunches. In this we also deserve that God deprive us of His Word and blessing, and again allow preachers of lies to arise to lead us to the devil, and, in addition, to drain our sweat and blood.

But those who keep in sight God's will and commandment have the promise that everything which they bestow upon temporal and spiritual fathers, and whatever they do to honor them, shall be richly recompensed to them, so that they shall have, not bread, clothing, and money for a year or two, but long life, support, and peace, and shall be eternally rich and blessed. Therefore only do what is your duty, and let God take care how He is to support you and provide for you sufficiently. Since He has promised it, and has never yet lied, He will not be found lying to you.

This ought indeed to encourage us, and give us hearts that would melt in pleasure and love toward those to whom we owe honor, so that we would raise our hands and joyfully thank God who has given us such promises, for which we ought to run to the ends of the world [to the remotest parts of India]. For although the whole world should combine, it could not add an hour to our life or give us a single grain from the earth. But God wishes to give you all exceeding abundantly according to your heart's desire. He who despises and casts this to the winds is not worthy ever to hear a word of God. This has now been stated more than enough for all who belong under this commandment.

In addition, it would be well to preach to the parents also, and such as bear their office, as to how they should deport themselves toward those who are committed to them for their government. For although this is not expressed in the Ten Commandments, it is nevertheless abundantly enjoined in many places in the Scriptures. And God desires to have it embraced in this commandment when He speaks of father and mother. For He does not wish to have in this office and government knaves and tyrants; nor does He assign to them this honor, that is, power and authority to govern, that they should have themselves worshiped; but they should consider that they are under obligations of obedience to God; and that, first of all, they should earnestly and faithfully discharge their office, not only to support and provide for the bodily necessities of their children, servants, subjects, etc., but, most of all, to train them to the honor and praise of God. Therefore do not think that this is left to your pleasure and arbitrary will, but that it is a strict command and injunction of God, to whom also you must give account for it.

But here again the sad plight arises that no one perceives or heeds this, and all live on as though God gave us children for our pleasure or amusement, and servants that we should employ them like a cow or ass, only for work, or as though we were only to gratify our wantonness with our subjects, ignoring them, as though it were no concern of ours what they learn or how they live; and no one is willing to see that this is the command of the Supreme Majesty, who will most strictly call us to account and punish us for it; nor that there is so great need to be so seriously concerned about the young. For if we wish to have excellent and apt persons both for civil and ecclesiastical government we must spare no diligence, time, or cost in teaching and educating our children, that they may serve God and the world, and we must not think only how we may amass money and possessions for them. For God can indeed without us support and make them rich, as He daily does. But for this purpose He has given us children, and issued this command that we should train and govern them according to His will, else He would have no need of father and mother. Let every one know therefore, that it is his duty, on peril of losing the divine favor, to bring up his children above all things in the fear and knowledge of God, and if they are talented, have them learn and study something, that they may be employed for whatever need there is [to have them instructed and trained in a liberal education, that men may be able to have their aid in government and in whatever is necessary].

If that were done, God would also richly bless us and give us grace to train men by whom land and people might be improved and likewise well educated citizens, chaste and domestic wives, who afterwards would rear godly children and servants. Here consider now what deadly injury you are doing if you be negligent and fail on your part to bring up your child to usefulness and piety, and how you bring upon yourself all sin and wrath, thus earning hell by your own children, even though you be otherwise pious and holy. And because this is disregarded, God so fearfully punishes the world that there is no discipline, government, or peace, of which we all complain, but do not see that it is our fault; for as we train them, we have spoiled and disobedient children and subjects. Let this be sufficient exhortation; for to draw this out at length belongs to another time.

The Fifth Commandment.

Thou shalt not kill.

We have now completed both the spiritual and the temporal government, that is, the divine and the paternal authority and obedience. But here now we go forth from our house among our neighbors to learn how we should live with one another, every one himself toward his neighbor. Therefore God and government are not included in this commandment nor is the power to kill, which they have taken away. For God has delegated His authority to punish evil-doers to the government instead of parents, who aforetime (as we read in Moses) were required to bring their own children to judgment and sentence them to death. Therefore, what is here forbidden is forbidden to the individual in his relation to any one else, and not to the government.

Now this commandment is easy enough and has been often treated, because we hear it annually in the Gospel of St. Matthew, 5, 21 ff., where Christ Himself explains and sums it up, namely, that we must not kill neither with hand, heart, mouth, signs, gestures, help, nor counsel. Therefore it is here forbidden to every one to be angry, except those (as we said) who are in the place of God, that is, parents and the government. For it is proper for God and for every one who is in a divine estate to be angry, to reprove and punish, namely, on account of those very persons who transgress this and the other commandments.

But the cause and need of this commandment is that God well knows that the world is evil, and that this life has much unhappiness; therefore He has placed this and the other commandments between the good and the evil. Now, as there are many assaults upon all commandments, so it happens also in this commandment that we must live among many people who do us harm, so that we have cause to be hostile to them.

As when your neighbor sees that you have a better house and home [a larger family and more fertile fields], greater possessions and fortune from God than he, he is sulky, envies you, and speaks no good of you.

Thus by the devil's incitement you will get many enemies who cannot bear to see you have any good, either bodily or spiritual. When we see such people, our hearts, in turn, would rage and bleed and take vengeance. Then there arise cursing and blows, from which follow finally misery and murder. Here, now, God like a kind father steps in ahead of Us, interposes and wishes to have the quarrel settled, that no misfortune come of it, nor one destroy another. And briefly He would hereby protect, set free, and keep in peace every one against the crime and violence of every one else; and would have this commandment placed as a wall, fortress, and refuge about our neighbor, that we do him no hurt nor harm in his body.

Thus this commandment aims at this, that no one offend his neighbor on account of any evil deed, even though he have fully deserved it. For where murder is forbidden, all cause also is forbidden whence murder may originate. For many a one, although he does not kill, yet curses and utters a wish, which would stop a person from running far if it were to strike him in the neck [makes imprecations, which if fulfilled with respect to any one, he would not live long]. Now since this inheres in every one by nature and it is a common practice that no one is willing to suffer at the hands of another, God wishes to remove the root and source by which the heart is embittered against our neighbor, and to accustom us ever to keep in view this commandment, always to contemplate ourselves in it as in a mirror, to regard the will of God, and with hearty confidence and invocation of His name to commit to Him the wrong which we suffer. Thus we shall suffer our enemies to rage and be angry, doing what they can, and we learn to calm our wrath, and to have a patient, gentle heart, especially toward those who give us cause to be angry, that is, our enemies.

Therefore the entire sum of what it means not to kill is to be impressed most explicitly upon the simple-minded. In the first place that we harm no one, first, with our hand or by deed. Then, that we do not employ our tongue to instigate or counsel thereto. Further, that we neither use nor assent to any kind of means or methods whereby any one may be injured. And finally, that the heart be not ill disposed toward any one, nor from anger and hatred wish him ill, so that body and soul may be innocent in regard to every one, but especially those who wish you evil or inflict such upon you. For to do evil to one who wishes and does you good is not human, but diabolical.

Secondly, under this commandment not only he is guilty who does evil to his neighbor, but he also who can do him good, prevent, resist evil, defend and save him, so that no bodily harm or hurt happen to him and yet does not do it. If, therefore, you send away one that is naked when you could clothe him, you have caused him to freeze to death; you see one suffer hunger and do not give him food, you have caused him to starve. So also, if you see any one innocently sentenced to death or in like distress, and do not save him, although you know ways and means to do so, you have killed him. And it will not avail you to make the pretext that you did not afford any help, counsel, or aid thereto for you have withheld your love from him and deprived him of the benefit whereby his life would have been saved.

Therefore God also rightly calls all those murderers who do not afford counsel and help in distress and danger of body and life, and will pass a most terrible sentence upon them in the last day, as Christ Himself has announced when He shall say, Matt.25, 42f.: I was an hungered, and ye gave Me no meat; I was thirsty, and ye gave Me no drink; I was a stranger, and ye took Me not in; naked, and ye clothed Me not; sick and in prison and ye visited Me not. That is: You would have suffered Me and Mine to die of hunger thirst, and cold, would have suffered the wild beasts to tear us to pieces, or left us to rot in prison or perish in distress. What else is that but to reproach them as murderers and bloodhounds? For although you have not actually done all this, you have nevertheless, so far as you were concerned, suffered him to pine and perish in misfortune.

It is just as if I saw some one navigating and laboring in deep water [and struggling against adverse winds] or one fallen into fire, and could extend to him the hand to pull him out and save him, and yet refused to do it. What else would I appear, even in the eyes of the world, than as a murderer and a criminal?

Therefore it is God's ultimate purpose that we suffer harm to befall no man, but show him all good and love; and, as we have said it is specially directed toward those who are our enemies. For to do good to our friends is but an ordinary heathen virtue as Christ says Matt. 5, 46.

Here we have again the Word of God whereby He would encourage and urge us to true noble and sublime works, as gentleness patience, and, in short, love and kindness to our enemies, and would ever remind us to reflect upon the First Commandment, that He is our God, that is, that He will help, assist, and protect us, in order that He may thus quench the desire of revenge in us.

This we ought to practice and inculcate and we would have our hands full doing good works. But this would not be preaching for monks; it would greatly detract from the religious estate, and infringe upon the sanctity of Carthusians, and would even be regarded as forbidding good works and clearing the convents. For in this wise the ordinary state of Christians would be considered just as worthy, and even worthier, and everybody would see how they mock and delude the world with a false, hypocritical show of holiness, because they have given this and other commandments to the winds, and have esteemed them unnecessary, as though they were not commandments but mere counsels, and have at the same time shamelessly proclaimed and boasted their hypocritical estate and works as the most perfect life, in order that they might lead a pleasant, easy life, without the cross and without patience, for which reason, too, they have resorted to the cloisters, so that they might not be obliged to suffer any wrong from any one or to do him any good. But know now that these are the true, holy, and godly works, in which, with all the angels He rejoices, in comparison with which all human holiness is but stench and filth, and besides, deserves nothing but wrath and damnation.

The Sixth Commandment.

Thou shalt not commit adultery.

These commandments now [that follow] are easily understood from [the explanation of] the preceding; for they are all to the effect that we [be careful to] avoid doing any kind of injury to our neighbor. But they are arranged in fine [elegant] order. In the first place, they treat of his own person. Then they proceed to the person nearest him, or the closest possession next after his body namely, his wife, who is one flesh and blood with him, so that we cannot inflict a higher injury upon him in any good that is his. Therefore it is explicitly forbidden here to bring any disgrace upon him in respect to his wife. And it really aims at adultery, because among the Jews it was ordained and commanded that every one must be married. Therefore also the young were early provided for [married], so that the virgin state was held in small esteem, neither were public prostitution and lewdness tolerated (as now). Therefore adultery was the most common form of unchastity among them.

But because among us there is such a shameful mess and the very dregs of all vice and lewdness, this commandment is directed also against all manner of unchastity, whatever it may be called; and not only is the external act forbidden, but also every kind of cause, incitement, and means, so that the heart, the lips, and the whole body may be chaste and afford no opportunity, help, or persuasion to unchastity. And not only this, but that we also make resistance, afford protection and rescue wherever there is danger and need; and again, that we give help and counsel, so as to maintain our neighbor's honor. For whenever you omit this when you could make resistance, or connive at it as if it did not concern you, you are as truly guilty as the one perpetrating the deed. Thus, to state it in the briefest manner, there is required this much, that every one both live chastely himself and help his neighbor do the same, so that God by this commandment wishes to hedge round about and protect [as with a rampart] every spouse that no one trespass against them.

But since this commandment is aimed directly at the state of matrimony and gives occasion to speak of the same, you must well understand and mark, first, how gloriously God honors and extols this estate, inasmuch as by His commandment He both sanctions and guards it. He has sanctioned it above in the Fourth Commandment: Honor thy father and thy mother; but here He has (as we said) hedged it about and protected it. Therefore He also wishes us to honor it, and to maintain and conduct it as a divine and blessed estate; because, in the first place, He has instituted it before all others, and therefore created man and woman separately (as is evident), not for lewdness, but that they should [legitimately] live together, be fruitful, beget children, and nourish and train them to the honor of God.

Therefore God has also most richly blessed this estate above all others, and, in addition, has bestowed on it and wrapped up in it everything in the world, to the end that this estate might be well and richly provided for. Married life is therefore no jest or presumption; but it is an excellent thing and a matter of divine seriousness. For it is of the highest importance to Him that persons be raised who may serve the world and promote the knowledge of God, godly living, and all virtues, to fight against wickedness and the devil.

Therefore I have always taught that this estate should not be despised nor held in disrepute, as is done by the blind world and our false ecclesiastics, but that it be regarded according to God's Word, by which it is adorned and sanctified, so that it is not only placed on an equality with other estates, but that it precedes and surpasses them all, whether they be that of emperor, princes, bishops, or whoever they please. For both ecclesiastical and civil estates must humble themselves and all be found in this estate as we shall hear. Therefore it is not a peculiar estate, but the most common and noblest estate, which pervades all Christendom, yea which extends through all the world.

In the second place, you must know also that it is not only an honorable, but also a necessary state, and it is solemnly commanded by God that, in general, in all conditions, men and women, who were created for it, shall be found in this estate; yet with some exceptions (although few) whom God has especially excepted, so that they are not fit for the married estate, or whom He has released by a high, supernatural gift that they can maintain chastity without this estate. For where nature has its course, as it is implanted by God, it is not possible to remain chaste without marriage. For flesh and blood remain flesh and blood, and the natural inclination and excitement have their course without let or hindrance, as everybody sees and feels. In order, therefore, that it may be the more easy in some degree to avoid unchastity, God has commanded the estate of matrimony, that every one may have his proper portion and be satisfied therewith; although God's grace besides is required in order that the heart also may be pure.

From this you see how this popish rabble, priests, monks, and nuns, resist

God's order and commandment, inasmuch as they despise and forbid matrimony, and presume and vow to maintain perpetual chastity, and, besides, deceive the simple-minded with lying words and appearances [impostures]. For no one has so little love and inclination to chastity as just those who because of great sanctity avoid marriage, and either indulge in open and shameless prostitution, or secretly do even worse, so that one dare not speak of it, as has, alas! been learned too fully. And, in short, even though they abstain from the act, their hearts are so full of unchaste thoughts and evil lusts that there is a continual burning and secret suffering, which can be avoided in the married life. Therefore all vows of chastity out of the married state are condemned by this commandment, and free permission is granted, yea, even the command is given, to all poor ensnared consciences which have been deceived by their monastic vows to abandon the unchaste state and enter the married life, considering that even if the monastic life were godly, it would nevertheless not be in their power to maintain chastity, and if they remain in it, they must only sin more and more against this commandment.

Now, I speak of this in order that the young may be so guided that they conceive a liking for the married estate, and know that it is a blessed estate and pleasing to God. For in this way we might in the course of time bring it about that married life be restored to honor, and that there might be less of the filthy, dissolute, disorderly doings which now run riot the world over in open prostitution and other shameful vices arising from disregard of married life. Therefore it is the duty of parents and the government to see to it that our youth be brought up to discipline and respectability, and when they have come to years of maturity, to provide for them [to have them married] in the fear of God and honorably; He would not fail to add His blessing and grace, so that men would have joy and happiness from the same.

Let me now say in conclusion that this commandment demands not only that every one live chastely in thought, word, and deed in his condition, that is, especially in the estate of matrimony, but also that every one love and esteem the spouse given him by God. For where conjugal chastity is to be maintained, man and wife must by all means live together in love and harmony, that one may cherish the other from the heart and with entire fidelity. For that is one of the principal points which enkindle love and desire of chastity, so that, where this is found, chastity will follow as a matter of course without any command. Therefore also St. Paul so diligently exhorts husband and wife to love and honor one another. Here you have again a precious, yea, many and great good works, of which you can joyfully boast, against all ecclesiastical estates, chosen without God's Word and commandment.

The Seventh Commandment.

Thou shalt not steal.

After your person and spouse temporal property comes next. That also God wishes to have protected, and He has commanded that no one shall subtract from, or curtail, his neighbor's possessions. For to steal is nothing else than to get possession of another's property wrongfully, which briefly comprehends all kinds of advantage in all sorts of trade to the disadvantage of our neighbor. Now, this is indeed quite a wide-spread and common vice, but so little regarded and observed that it exceeds all measure, so that if all who are thieves, and yet do not wish to be called such, were to be hanged on gallows the world would soon be devastated and there would be a lack both of executioners and gallows. For, as we have just said, to steal is to signify not only to empty our neighbor's coffer and pockets, but to be grasping in the market, in all stores, booths, wine- and beer-cellars, workshops, and, in short, wherever there is trading or taking and giving of money for merchandise or labor.

As, for instance, to explain this somewhat grossly for the common people, that it may be seen how godly we are: When a manservant or maid-servant does not serve faithfully in the house, and does damage, or allows it to be done when it could be prevented, or otherwise ruins and neglects the goods entrusted to him, from indolence idleness, or malice, to the spite and vexation of master and mistress, and in whatever way this can be done purposely (for I do not speak of what happens from oversight and against one's will), you can in a year abscond thirty, forty florins, which if another had taken secretly or carried away, he would be hanged with the rope. But here you [while conscious of such a great theft] may even bid defiance and become insolent, and no one dare call you a thief.

The same I say also of mechanics, workmen, and day-laborers, who all follow their wanton notions, and never know enough ways to overcharge people, while they are lazy and unfaithful in their work. All these are far worse than sneak-thieves, against whom we can guard with locks and bolts, or who, if apprehended, are treated in such a manner that they will not do the same again. But against these no one can guard, no one dare even look awry at them or accuse them of theft, so that one would ten times rather lose from his purse. For here are my neighbors, good friends, my own servants, from whom I expect good [every faithful and diligent service], who defraud me first of all.

Furthermore, in the market and in common trade likewise, this practice is in full swing and force to the greatest extent, where one openly defrauds another with bad merchandise, false measures, weights, coins, and by nimbleness and queer finances or dexterous tricks takes advantage of him; likewise, when one overcharges a person in a trade and wantonly drives a hard bargain, skins and distresses him. And who can recount or think of all these things? To sum up, this is the commonest craft and the largest guild on earth, and if we regard the world throughout all conditions of life, it is nothing else than a vast, wide stall, full of great thieves.

Therefore they are also called swivel-chair robbers, land- and highway-robbers, not pick-locks and sneak-thieves who snatch away the ready cash, but who sit on the chair [at home] and are styled great noblemen, and honorable, pious citizens, and yet rob and steal under a good pretext.

Yes, here we might be silent about the trifling individual thieves if we were to attack the great, powerful arch-thieves with whom lords and princes keep company, who daily plunder not only a city or two, but all Germany. Yea, where should we place the head and supreme protector of all thieves, the Holy Chair at Rome with all its retinue, which has grabbed by theft the wealth of all the world, and holds it to this day?

This is, in short, the course of the world: whoever can steal and rob openly goes free and secure, unmolested by any one, and even demands that he be honored. Meanwhile the little sneak-thieves, who have once trespassed, must bear the shame and punishment to render the former godly and honorable. But let them know that in the sight of God they are the greatest thieves, and that He will punish them as they are worthy and deserve.

Now, since this commandment is so far-reaching [and comprehensive], as just indicated, it is necessary to urge it well and to explain it to the common people, not to let them go on in their wantonness and security, but always to place before their eyes the wrath of God, and inculcate the same. For we have to preach this not to Christians, but chiefly to knaves and scoundrels, to whom it would be more fitting for judges, jailers, or Master Hannes [the executioner] to preach. Therefore let every one know that it is his duty, at the risk of God's displeasure, not only to do no injury to his neighbor, nor to deprive him of gain, nor to perpetrate any act of unfaithfulness or malice in any bargain or trade, but faithfully to preserve his property for him, to secure and promote his advantage, especially when one accepts money, wages, and one's livelihood for such service.

He now who wantonly despises this may indeed pass along and escape the hangman, but he shall not escape the wrath and punishment of God; and when he has long practiced his defiance and arrogance, he shall yet remain a tramp and beggar, and, in addition, have all plagues and misfortune. Now you are going your way [wherever your heart's pleasure calls you] while you ought to preserve the property of your master and mistress, for which service you fill your crop and maw, take your wages like a thief, have people treat you as a nobleman; for there are many that are even insolent towards their masters and mistresses, and are unwilling to do them a favor or service by which to protect them from loss.

But reflect what you will gain when, having come into your own property and being set up in your home (to which God will help with all misfortunes), it [your perfidy] will bob up again and come home to you, and you will find that where you have cheated or done injury to the value of one mite, you will have to pay thirty again.

Such shall be the lot also of mechanics and day-laborers of whom we are now obliged to hear and suffer such intolerable maliciousness, as though they were noblemen in another's possessions, and every one were obliged to give them what they demand. Just let them continue practicing their exactions as long as they can; but God will not forget His commandment, and will reward them according as they have served, and will hang them, not upon a green gallows, but upon a dry one so that all their life they shall neither prosper nor accumulate anything. And indeed, if there were a well-ordered government in the land, such wantonness might soon be checked and prevented, as was the custom in ancient times among the Romans, where such characters were promptly seized by the pate in a way that others took warning.

No more shall all the rest prosper who change the open free market into a carrion-pit of extortion and a den of robbery, where the poor are daily overcharged, new burdens and high prices are imposed, and every one uses the market according to his caprice, and is even defiant and brags as though it were his fair privilege and right to sell his goods for as high a price as he please, and no one had a right to say a word against it. We will indeed look on and let these people skin, pinch, and hoard, but we will trust in God — who will, however, do this of His own accord, — that, after you have been skinning and scraping for a long time, He will pronounce such a blessing on your gains that your grain in the garner, your beer in the cellar, your cattle in the stalls shall perish; yea, where you have cheated and overcharged any one to the amount of a florin, your entire pile shall be consumed with rust, so that you shall never enjoy it.

And indeed, we see and experience this being fulfilled daily before our eyes, that no stolen or dishonestly acquired possession thrives. How many there are who rake and scrape day and night, and yet grow not a farthing richer! And though they gather much, they must suffer so many plagues and misfortunes that they cannot relish it with cheerfulness nor transmit it to their children. But as no one minds it, and we go on as though it did not concern us, God must visit us in a different way and teach us manners by imposing one taxation after another, or billeting a troop of soldiers upon us, who in one hour empty our coffers and purses, and do not quit as long as we have a farthing left, and in addition, by way of thanks, burn and devastate house and home, and outrage and kill wife and children.

And, in short, if you steal much, depend upon it that again as much will be stolen from you; and he who robs and acquires with violence and wrong will submit to one who shall deal after the same fashion with him. For God is master of this art, that since every one robs and steals from the other, He punishes one thief by means of another. Else where should we find enough gallows and ropes?

Now, whoever is willing to be instructed let him know that this is the commandment of God, and that it must not be treated as a jest. For although you despise us, defraud, steal, and rob, we will indeed manage to endure your haughtiness, suffer, and, according to the Lord's Prayer, forgive and show pity; for we know that the godly shall nevertheless have enough, and you injure yourself more than another.

But beware of this: When the poor man comes to you (of whom there are so many now) who must buy with the penny of his daily wages and live upon it, and you are harsh to him, as though every one lived by your favor, and you skin and scrape to the bone, and, besides, with pride and haughtiness turn him off to whom you ought to give for nothing, he will go away wretched and sorrowful, and since he can complain to no one he will cry and call to heaven, — then beware (I say again) as of the devil himself. For such groaning and calling will be no jest, but will have a weight that will prove too heavy for you and all the world. For it will reach Him who takes care of the poor sorrowful hearts, and will not allow them to go unavenged. But if you despise this and become defiant, see whom you have brought upon you: if you succeed and prosper, you may before all the world call God and me a liar.

We have exhorted, warned, and protested enough; he who will not heed or believe it may go on until he learns this by experience Yet it must be impressed upon the young that they may be careful not to follow the old lawless crowd, but keep their eyes fixed upon God's commandment, lest His wrath and punishment come upon them too. It behooves us to do no more than to instruct and reprove with God's Word; but to check such open wantonness there is need of the princes and government, who themselves would have eyes and the courage to establish and maintain order in all manner of trade and commerce, lest the poor be burdened and oppressed nor they themselves be loaded with other men's sins.

Let this suffice as an explanation of what stealing is, that it be not taken too narrowly but made to extend as far as we have to do with our neighbors. And briefly, in a summary, as in the former commandments, it is herewith forbidden, in the first place, to do our neighbor any injury or wrong (in whatever manner supposable, by curtailing, forestalling, and withholding his possessions and property), or even to consent or allow such a thing, but to interpose and prevent it. And, on the other hand, it is commanded that we advance and improve his possessions, and in case he suffers want, that we help, communicate, and lend both to friends and foes.

Whoever now seeks and desires good works will find here more than enough such as are heartily acceptable and pleasing to God, and in addition are favored and crowned with excellent blessings, that we are to be richly compensated for all that we do for our neighbor's good and from friendship; as King Solomon also teaches Prov. 19, 17: He that hath pity upon the poor lendeth unto the Lord; and that which he hath given will He pay him again. Here, then you have a rich Lord, who is certainly sufficient for you, and who will not suffer you to come short in anything or to want; thus you can with a joyful conscience enjoy a hundred times more than you could scrape together with unfaithfulness and wrong. Now, whoever does not desire the blessing will find wrath and misfortune enough.

The Eighth Commandment.

Thou shalt not bear false witness against thy neighbor.

Over and above our own body, spouse, and temporal possessions, we have yet another treasure, namely, honor and good report [the illustrious testimony of an upright and unsullied name and reputation], with which we cannot dispense. For it is intolerable to live among men in open shame and general contempt. Therefore God wishes the reputation, good name, and upright character of our neighbor to be taken away or diminished as little as his money and possessions, that every one may stand in his integrity before wife, children, servants, and neighbors. And in the first place, we take the plainest meaning of this commandment according to the words (Thou shalt not bear false witness), as pertaining to the public courts of justice, where a poor innocent man is accused and oppressed by false witnesses in order to be punished in his body, property, or honor.

Now, this appears as if it were of little concern to us at present; but with the Jews it was quite a common and ordinary matter. For the people were organized under an excellent and regular government; and where there is still such a government, instances of this sin will not be wanting. The cause of it is that where judges, burgomasters, princes, or others in authority sit in judgment, things never fail to go according to the course of the world; namely, men do not like to offend anybody, flatter, and speak to gain favor, money, prospects, or friendship; and in consequence a poor man and his cause must be oppressed, denounced as wrong, and suffer punishment. And it is a common calamity in the world that in courts of justice there seldom preside godly men.

For to be a judge requires above all things a godly man, and not only a godly, but also a wise, modest, yea, a brave and bold man; likewise, to be a witness requires a fearless and especially a godly man. For a person who is to judge all matters rightly and carry them through with his decision will often offend good friends, relatives, neighbors, and the rich and powerful, who can greatly serve or injure him. Therefore he must be quite blind, have his eyes and ears closed, neither see nor hear, but go straight forward in everything that comes before him, and decide accordingly.

Therefore this commandment is given first of all that every one shall help his neighbor to secure his rights, and not allow them to be hindered or twisted, but shall promote and strictly maintain them, no matter whether he be judge or witness, and let it pertain to whatsoever it will. And especially is a goal set up here for our jurists that they be careful to deal truly and uprightly with every case, allowing right to remain right, and, on the other hand, not perverting anything [by their tricks and technical points turning black into white and making wrong out to be right], nor glossing it over or keeping silent concerning it, irrespective of a person's money, possession, honor, or power. This is one part and the plainest sense of this commandment concerning all that takes place in court.

Next, it extends very much further, if we are to apply it to spiritual jurisdiction or administration; here it is a common occurrence that every one bears false witness against his neighbor. For wherever there are godly preachers and Christians, they must bear the sentence before the world that they are called heretics, apostates, yea, seditious and desperately wicked miscreants. Besides the Word of God must suffer in the most shameful and malicious manner, being persecuted blasphemed, contradicted, perverted and falsely cited and interpreted. But let this pass; for it is the way of the blind world that she condemns and persecutes the truth and the children of God, and yet esteems it no sin.

In the third place, what concerns us all, this commandment forbids all sins of the tongue whereby we may injure or approach too closely to our neighbor. For to bear false witness is nothing else than a work of the tongue. Now, whatever is done with the tongue against a fellow-man God would have prohibited, whether it be false preachers with their doctrine and blasphemy, false judges and witnesses with their verdict, or outside of court by lying and evil-speaking. Here belongs particularly the detestable, shameful vice of speaking behind a person's back and slandering, to which the devil spurs us on and of which there would be much to be said. For it is a common evil plague that every one prefers hearing evil to hearing good of his neighbor; and although we ourselves are so bad that we cannot suffer that any one should say anything bad about us, but every one would much rather that all the world should speak of him in terms of gold, yet we cannot bear that the best is spoken about others.

Therefore, to avoid this vice we should note that no one is allowed publicly to judge and reprove his neighbor, although he may see him sin, unless he have a command to judge and to reprove. For there is a great difference between these two things, judging sin and knowing sin. You may indeed know it, but you are not to judge it. I can indeed see and hear that my neighbor sins, but I have no command to report it to others. Now, if I rush in, judging and passing sentence, I fall into a sin which is greater than his. But if you know it, do nothing else than turn your ears into a grave and cover it, until you are appointed to be judge and to punish by virtue of your office.

Those, then, are called slanderers who are not content with knowing a thing, but proceed to assume jurisdiction, and when they know a slight offense of another, carry it into every corner, and are delighted and tickled that they can stir up another's displeasure [baseness], as swine roll themselves in the dirt and root in it with the snout. This is nothing else than meddling with the judgment and office of God, and pronouncing sentence and punishment with the most severe verdict. For no judge can punish to a higher degree nor go farther than to say: "He is a thief, a murderer, a traitor," etc. Therefore, whoever presumes to say the same of his neighbor goes just as far as the emperor and all governments. For although you do not wield the sword, you employ your poisonous tongue to the shame and hurt of your neighbor.

God therefore would have it prohibited that any one speak evil of another even though he be guilty, and the latter know it right well; much less if he do not know it, and have it only from hearsay. But you say: Shall I not say it if it be the truth? Answer: Why do you not make accusation to regular judges? Ah, I cannot prove it publicly, and hence I might be silenced and turned away in a harsh manner [incur the penalty of a false accusation]. "Ah, indeed, do you smell the roast?" If you do not trust yourself to stand before the proper authorities and to make answer, then hold your tongue. But if you know it, know it for yourself and not for another. For if you tell it to others, although it be true, you will appear as a liar, because you cannot prove it, and you are, besides acting like a knave. For we ought never to deprive any one of his honor or good name unless it be first taken away from him publicly.

False witness, then, is everything which cannot be properly proved. Therefore, what is not manifest upon sufficient evidence no one shall make public or declare for truth; and in short, whatever is secret should be allowed to remain secret, or, at any rate, should be secretly reproved, as we shall hear. Therefore, if you encounter an idle tongue which betrays and slanders some one, contradict such a one promptly to his face, that he may blush thus many a one will hold his tongue who else would bring some poor man into bad repute from which he would not easily extricate himself. For honor and a good name are easily taken away, but not easily restored.

Thus you see that it is summarily forbidden to speak any evil of our neighbor, however the civil government, preachers, father and mother excepted, on the understanding that this commandment does not allow evil to go unpunished. Now, as according to the Fifth Commandment no one is to be injured in body, and yet Master Hannes [the executioner] is excepted, who by virtue of his office does his neighbor no good, but only evil and harm, and nevertheless does not sin against God's commandment, because God has on His own account instituted that office; for He has reserved punishment for His own good pleasure, as He threatens in the First Commandment, — just so also, although no one has a right in his own person to judge and condemn anybody, yet if they to whose office it belongs fail to do it, they sin as well as he who would do so of his own accord, without such office. For here necessity requires one to speak of the evil, to prefer charges, to investigate and testify; and it is not different from the case of a physician who is sometimes compelled to examine and handle the patient whom he is to cure in secret parts. Just so governments, father and mother, brothers and sisters, and other good friends, are under obligation to each other to reprove evil wherever it is needful and profitable.

But the true way in this matter would be to observe the order according to the Gospel, Matt. 18, 15, where Christ says: If thy brother shall trespass against thee, go and tell him his fault between thee and him alone. Here you have a precious and excellent teaching for governing well the tongue, which is to be carefully observed against this detestable misuse. Let this, then, be your rule, that you do not too readily spread evil concerning your neighbor and slander him to others, but admonish him privately that he may amend [his life]. Likewise, also, if some one report to you what this or that one has done, teach him, too, to go and admonish him personally if he have seen it himself; but if not, that he hold his tongue.

The same you can learn also from the daily government of the household. For when the master of the house sees that the servant does not do what he ought, he admonishes him personally. But if he were so foolish as to let the servant sit at home, and went on the streets to complain of him to his neighbors, he would no doubt be told: "You fool, what does that concern us? Why do you not tell it to him ?" Behold, that would be acting quite brotherly, so that the evil would be stayed, and your neighbor would retain his honor. As Christ also says in the same place: If he hear thee, thou host gained thy brother. Then you have done a great and excellent work; for do you think it is a little matter to gain a brother? Let all monks and holy orders step forth, with all their works melted together into one mass, and see if they can boast that they have gained a brother.

Further, Christ teaches: But if he will not hear thee, then take with thee one or two more, that in the mouth of two or three witnesses every word may be established. So he whom it concerns is always to be treated with personally, and not to be spoken of without his knowledge. But if that do not avail, then bring it publicly before the community, whether before the civil or the ecclesiastical tribunal. For then you do not stand alone, but you have those witnesses with you by whom you can convict the guilty one, relying on whom the judge can pronounce sentence and punish. This is the right and regular course for checking and reforming a wicked person. But if we gossip about another in all corners and stir the filth, no one will be reformed, and afterwards when we are to stand up and bear witness, we deny having said so. Therefore it would serve such tongues right if their itch for slander were severely punished, as a warning to others. If you were acting for your neighbor's reformation or from love of the truth, you would not sneak about secretly nor shun the day and the light.

All this has been said regarding secret sins. But where the sin is quite public so that the judge and everybody know it you can without any sin avoid him and let him go, because he has brought himself into disgrace, and you may also publicly testify concerning him. For when a matter is public in the light of day, there can be no slandering or false judging or testifying; as, when we now reprove the Pope with his doctrine, which is publicly set forth in books and proclaimed in all the world. For where the sin is public, the reproof also must be public, that every one may learn to guard against it.

Thus we have now the sum and general understanding of this commandment, to wit, that no one do any injury with the tongue to his neighbor, whether friend or foe, nor speak evil of him, no matter whether it be true or false, unless it be done by commandment or for his reformation, but that every one employ his tongue and make it serve for the best of every one else, to cover up his neighbor's sins and infirmities, excuse them, palliate and garnish them with his own reputation. The chief reason for this should be the one which Christ alleges in the Gospel, in which He comprehends all commandments respecting our neighbor, Matt. 7, 12: Whatsoever ye would that men should do to you, do ye even so to them.

Even nature teaches the same thing in our own bodies, as St. Paul says, 1 Cor. 12, 22: Much more, those members of the body which seem to be more feeble are necessary; and those members of the body which we think to be less honorable, upon these we bestow more abundant honor; and our uncomely parts have more abundant comeliness. No one covers his face, eyes, nose, and mouth, for they, being in themselves the most honorable members which we have, do not require it. But the most infirm members, of which we are ashamed, we cover with all diligence; hands, eyes, and the whole body must help to cover and conceal them. Thus also among ourselves should we adorn whatever blemishes and infirmities we find in our neighbor, and serve and help him to promote his honor to the best of our ability, and, on the other hand, prevent whatever may be discreditable to him. And it is especially an excellent and noble virtue for one always to explain advantageously and put the best construction upon all he may hear of his neighbor (if it be not notoriously evil), or at any rate to condone it over and against the poisonous tongues that are busy wherever they can pry out and discover something to blame in a neighbor, and that explain and pervert it in the worst way; as is done now especially with the precious Word of God and its preachers.

There are comprehended therefore in this commandment quite a multitude of good works which please God most highly, and bring abundant good and blessing, if only the blind world and the false saints would recognize them. For there is nothing on or in entire man which can do both greater and more extensive good or harm in spiritual and in temporal matters than the tongue, though it is the least and feeblest member.

The Ninth and Tenth Commandments

Thou shalt not covet thy neighbor's house. Thou shalt not covet thy neighbor's wife, nor his man-servant, nor his maid-servant, nor his cattle, nor anything that is his.

These two commandments are given quite exclusively to the Jews; nevertheless, in part they also concern us. For they do not interpret them as referring to unchastity or theft, because these are sufficiently forbidden above. They also thought that they had kept all those when they had done or not done the external act. Therefore God has added these two commandments in order that it be esteemed as sin and forbidden to desire or in any way to aim at getting our neighbor's wife or possessions; and especially because under the Jewish government man-servants and maid-servants were not free as now to serve for wages as long as they pleased, but were their master's property with their body and all they had, as cattle and other possessions. Moreover, every man had power over his wife to put her away publicly by giving her a bill of divorce, and to take another. Therefore they were in constant danger among each other that if one took a fancy to another's wife, he might allege any reason both to dismiss his own wife and to estrange the other's wife from him, that he might obtain her under pretext of right. That was not considered a sin nor disgrace with them; as little as now with hired help, when a proprietor dismisses his man-servant or maid-servant, or takes another's servants from him in any way.

Therefore (I say) they thus interpreted these commandments, and that rightly (although their scope reaches somewhat farther and higher), that no one think or purpose to obtain what belongs to another, such as his wife, servants, house and estate, land meadows, cattle, even with a show of right or by a subterfuge, yet with injury to his neighbor. For above, in the Seventh Commandment, the vice is forbidden where one wrests to himself the possessions of others, or withholds them from his neighbor, which he cannot do by right. But here it is also forbidden to alienate anything from your neighbor, even though you could do so with honor in the eyes of the world, so that no one could accuse or blame you as though you had obtained it wrongfully.

For we are so inclined by nature that no one desires to see another have as much as himself, and each one acquires as much as he can; the other may fare as best he can. And yet we pretend to be godly, know how to adorn ourselves most finely and conceal our rascality, resort to and invent adroit devices and deceitful artifices (such as now are daily most ingeniously contrived) as though they were derived from the law codes; yea, we even dare impertinently to refer to it, and boast of it, and will not have it called rascality, but shrewdness and caution. In this lawyers and jurists assist, who twist and stretch the law to suit it to their cause, stress words and use them for a subterfuge, irrespective of equity or their neighbor's necessity. And, in short, whoever is the most expert and cunning in these affairs finds most help in law, as they themselves say: Vigilantibus iura subveniunt [that is, The laws favor the watchful].

This last commandment therefore is given not for rogues in the eyes of the world, but just for the most pious, who wish to be praised and be called honest and upright people, since they have not offended against the former commandments, as especially the Jews claimed to be, and even now many great noblemen, gentlemen, and princes. For the other common masses belong yet farther down, under the Seventh Commandment, as those who are not much concerned whether they acquire their possessions with honor and right.

Now, this occurs most frequently in cases that are brought into court, where it is the purpose to get something from our neighbor and to force him out of his own. As (to give examples), when people quarrel and wrangle about a large inheritance, real estate, etc., they avail themselves of, and resort to, whatever has the appearance of right, so dressing and adorning everything that the law must favor their side, and they keep the property with such title that no one can make complaint or lay claim thereto. In like manner, if any one desire to have a castle, city, duchy, or any other great thing, he practises so much financiering through relationships, and by any means he can, that the other is judicially deprived of it, and it is adjudicated to him, and confirmed with deed and seal and declared to have been acquired by princely title and honestly.

Likewise also in common trade where one dexterously slips something out of another's hand, so that he must look after it, or surprises and defrauds him in a matter in which he sees advantage and benefit for himself, so that the latter, perhaps on account of distress or debt, cannot regain or redeem it without injury, and the former gains the half or even more; and yet this must not be considered as acquired by fraud or stolen, but honestly bought. Here they say: First come, first served, and every one must look to his own interest, let another get what he can. And who can be so smart as to think of all the ways in which one can get many things into his possession by such specious pretexts? This the world does not consider wrong [nor is it punished by laws], and will not see that the neighbor is thereby placed at a disadvantage, and must sacrifice what he cannot spare without injury. Yet there is no one who wishes this to be done to him; from which we can easily perceive that such devices and pretexts are false.

Thus it was done formerly also with respect to wives: they knew such devices that if one were pleased with another woman, he personally or through others (as there were many ways and means to be invented) caused her husband to conceive a displeasure toward her, or had her resist him and so conduct herself that he was obliged to dismiss her and leave her to the other. That sort of thing undoubtedly prevailed much under the Law, as also we read in the (Gospel of King Herod that he took his brother's wife while he was yet living, and yet wished to be thought an honorable, pious man, as St. Mark also testifies of him. But such an example, I trust, will not occur among us, because in the New Testament those who are married are forbidden to be divorced, except in such a case where one [shrewdly] by some stratagem takes away a rich bride from another. But it is not a rare thing with us that one estranges or alienates another's man-servant or maid-servant, or entices them away by flattering words.

In whatever way such things happen, we must know that God does not wish that you deprive your neighbor of anything that belongs to him so that he suffer the loss and you gratify your avarice with it, even if you could keep it honorably before the world; for it is a secret and insidious imposition practised under the hat, as we say, that it may not be observed. For although you go your way as if you had done no one any wrong, you have nevertheless injured your neighbor; and if it is not called stealing and cheating, yet it is called coveting your neighbor's property, that is, aiming at possession of it, enticing it away from him without his will, and being unwilling to see him enjoy what God has granted him. And although the judge and every one must leave you in possession of it, yet God will not leave you therein; for He sees the deceitful heart and the malice of the world, which is sure to take an ell in addition wherever you yield to her a finger's breadth, and at length public wrong and violence follow.

Therefore we allow these commandments to remain in their ordinary meaning, that it is commanded, first, that we do not desire our neighbor's damage, nor even assist, nor give occasion for it, but gladly wish and leave him what he has, and, besides, advance and preserve for him what may be for his profit and service, as we should wish to be treated. Thus these commandments are especially directed against envy and miserable avarice, God wishing to remove all causes and sources whence arises everything by which we do injury to our neighbor, and therefore He expresses it in plain words: Thou shalt not covet, etc. For He would especially have the heart pure, although we shall never attain to that as long as we live here; so that this commandment will remain, like all the rest, one that will constantly accuse us and show how godly we are in the sight of God!

Conclusion of the Ten Commandments.

Thus we have the Ten Commandments, a compend of divine doctrine, as to what we are to do in order that our whole life may be pleasing to God, and the true fountain and channel from and in which everything must arise and flow that is to be a good work, so that outside of the Ten Commandments no work or thing can be good or pleasing to God, however great or precious it be in the eyes of the world. Let us see now what our great saints can boast of their spiritual orders and their great and grievous works which they have invented and set up, while they let these pass, as though they were far too insignificant, or had long ago been perfectly fulfilled.

I am of opinion indeed, that here one will find his hands full, [and will have enough] to do to observe these, namely, meekness, patience, and love towards enemies, chastity, kindness, etc., and what such virtues imply. But such works are not of value and make no display in the eyes of the world; for they are not peculiar and conceited works and restricted to particular times, places, rites, and customs, but are common, every-day domestic works which one neighbor can practise toward another; therefore they are not of high esteem.

But the other works cause people to open their eyes and ears wide, and men aid to this effect by the great display, expense, and magnificent buildings with which they adorn them, so that everything shines and glitters. There they waft incense, they sing and ring bells, they light tapers and candles, so that nothing else can be seen or heard. For when a priest stands there in a surplice embroidered with gilt, or a layman continues all day upon his knees in church, that is regarded as a most precious work which no one can sufficiently praise. But when a poor girl tends a little child and faithfully does what she is told that is considered nothing; for else what should monks and nuns seek in their cloisters?

But see, is not that a cursed presumption of those desperate saints who dare to invent a higher and better life and estate than the Ten Commandments teach, pretending (as we have said) that this is an ordinary life for the common man, but that theirs is for saints and perfect ones? And the miserable blind people do not see that no man can get so far as to keep one of the Ten Commandments as it should be kept, but both the Apostles' Creed and the Lord's Prayer must come to our aid (as we shall hear), by which that [power and strength to keep the commandments] is sought and prayed for and received continually. Therefore all their boasting amounts to as much as if I boasted and said: To be sure, I have not a penny to make payment with, but I confidently undertake to pay ten florins.

All this I say and urge in order that men might become rid of the sad misuse which has taken such deep root and still cleaves to everybody, and in all estates upon earth become used to looking hither only, and to being concerned about these matters. For it will be a long time before they will produce a doctrine or estates equal to the Ten Commandments, because they are so high that no one can attain to them by human power; and whoever does attain to them is a heavenly, angelic man far above all holiness of the world. Only occupy yourself with them, and try your best, apply all power and ability and you will find so much to do that you will neither seek nor esteem any other work or holiness.

Let this be sufficient concerning the first part of the common Christian doctrine, both for teaching and urging what is necessary. In conclusion, however, we must repeat the text which belongs here, of which we have treated already in the First Commandment, in order that we may learn what pains God requires to the end we may learn to inculcate and practise the Ten Commandments:

For I the Lord, thy God, am a jealous God, visiting the iniquity of the fathers upon the children unto the third and fourth generation of them that hate Me, and showing mercy unto thousands of them that love Me and keep My commandments.

Although (as we have heard above) this appendix was primarily attached to the First Commandment, it was nevertheless [we cannot deny that it was] laid down for the sake of all the commandments, as all of them are to be referred and directed to it. Therefore I have said that this, too, should be presented to and inculcated upon the young, that they may learn and remember it, in order to see what is to urge and compel us to keep these Ten Commandments. And it is to be regarded as though this part were specially added to each, so that it inheres in, and pervades, them all.

Now, there is comprehended in these words (as said before) both an angry word of threatening and a friendly promise to terrify and warn us, and, moreover to induce and encourage us to receive and highly esteem His Word as a matter of divine earnestness, because He Himself declares how much He is concerned about it, and how rigidly He will enforce it, namely, that He will horribly and terribly punish all who despise and transgress His commandments; and again, how richly He will reward, bless, and do all good to those who hold them in high esteem, and gladly do and live according to them. Thus He demands that all our works proceed from a heart which fears and regards God alone, and from such fear avoids everything that is contrary to His will, lest it should move Him to wrath; and, on the other hand, also trusts in Him alone, and from love to Him does all He wishes, because he speaks to us as friendly as a father, and offers us all grace and every good.

Just this is also the meaning and true interpretation of the first and chief commandment, from which all the others must flow and proceed, so that this word: Thou shalt have no other gods before Me, in its simplest meaning states nothing else than this demand: Thou shalt fear, love, and trust in Me as thine only true God. For where there is a heart thus disposed towards God, the same has fulfilled this and all the other commandments. On the other hand, whoever fears and loves anything else in heaven and upon earth will keep neither this nor any. Thus the entire scriptures have everywhere preached and inculcated this commandment, aiming always at these two things: fear of God and trust in Him. And especially the prophet David throughout the Psalms, as when he says [Ps. 147,11]: The Lord taketh pleasure in them that fear Him, in those that hope in His mercy. As if the entire commandment were explained by one verse, as much as to say: The Lord taketh pleasure in those who have no other gods.

Thus the First Commandment is to shine and impart its splendor to all the others. Therefore you must let this declaration run through all the commandments, like a hoop in a wreath, joining the end to the beginning and holding them all together, that it be continually repeated and not forgotten; as, namely, in the Second Commandment, that we fear God and do not take His name in vain for cursing, lying, deceiving, and other modes of leading men astray, or rascality, but make proper and good use of it by calling upon Him in prayer, praise, and thanksgiving, derived from love and trust according to the First Commandment. In like manner such fear, love, and trust is to urge and force us not to despise His Word, but gladly to learn, hear, and esteem it holy, and honor it.

Thus continuing through all the following commandments towards our neighbor likewise, everything is to proceed by virtue of the First Commandment, to wit, that we honor father and mother, masters, and all in authority and be subject and obedient to them, not on their own account, but for God's sake. For you are not to regard or fear father or mother, or from love of them do or omit anything. But see to that which God would have you do, and what He will quite surely demand of you; if you omit that, you have an angry Judge, but in the contrary case a gracious Father.

Again, that you do your neighbor no harm, injury, or violence, nor in any wise encroach upon him as touching his body, wife, property, honor, or rights, as all these things are commanded in their order, even though you have opportunity and cause to do so and no man would reprove you; but that you do good to all men, help them, and promote their interest, howsoever and wherever you can, purely from love of God and in order to please Him, in the confidence that He will abundantly reward you for everything. Thus you see how the First Commandment is the chief source and fountainhead which flows into all the rest, and again, all return to that and depend upon it, so that beginning and end are fastened and bound to each other.

This (I say) it is profitable and necessary always to teach to the young people, to admonish them and to remind them of it, that they may be brought up not only with blows and compulsion, like cattle, but in the fear and reverence of God. For where this is considered and laid to heart that these things are not human trifles, but the commandments of the Divine Majesty, who insists upon them with such earnestness, is angry with, and punishes those who despise them, and, on the other hand, abundantly rewards those who keep them, there will be a spontaneous impulse and a desire gladly to do the will of God. Therefore it is not in vain that it is commanded in the Old Testament to write the Ten Commandments on all walls and corners, yes, even on the garments, not for the sake of merely having them written in these places and making a show of them, as did the Jews, but that we might have our eyes constantly fixed upon them, and have them always in our memory, and that we might practise them in all our actions and ways, and every one make them his daily exercise in all cases, in every business and transaction, as though they were written in every place wherever he would look, yea, wherever he walks or stands. Thus there would be occasion enough, both at home in our own house and abroad with our neighbors, to practise the Ten Commandments, that no one need run far for them.

From this it again appears how highly these Ten Commandments are to be exalted and extolled above all estates, commandments, and works which are taught and practised aside from them. For here we can boast and say: Let all the wise and saints step forth and produce, if they can, a [single] work like these commandments, upon which God insists with such earnestness, and which He enjoins with His greatest wrath and punishment, and, besides, adds such glorious promises that He will pour out upon us all good things and blessings. Therefore they should be taught above all others, and be esteemed precious and dear, as the highest treasure given by God.

Part Second. Of the Creed.

Thus far we have heard the first part of Christian doctrine, in which we have seen all that God wishes us to do or to leave undone. Now, there properly follows the Creed, which sets forth to us everything that we must expect and receive from God, and, to state it quite briefly, teaches us to know Him fully. And this is intended to help us do that which according to the Ten Commandments we ought to do. For (as said above) they are set so high that all human ability is far too feeble and weak to [attain to or] keep them. Therefore it is as necessary to learn this part as the former in order that we may know how to attain thereto, whence and whereby to obtain such power. For if we could by our own powers keep the Ten Commandments as they are to be kept, we would need nothing further, neither the Creed nor the Lord's Prayer. But before we explain this advantage and necessity of the Creed, it is sufficient at first for the simple-minded that they learn to comprehend and understand the Creed itself.

In the first place, the Creed has hitherto been divided into twelve articles, although, if all points which are written in the Scriptures and which belong to the Creed were to be distinctly set forth, there would be far more articles, nor could they all be clearly expressed in so few words. But that it may be most easily and clearly understood as it is to be taught to children, we shall briefly sum up the entire Creed in three chief articles, according to the three persons in the Godhead, to whom everything that we believe is related, So that the First Article, of God the Father, explains Creation, the Second Article, of the Son, Redemption, and the Third, of the Holy Ghost, Sanctification. Just as though the Creed were briefly comprehended in so many words: I believe in God the Father, who has created me; I believe in God the Son, who has redeemed me; I believe in the Holy Ghost, who sanctifies me. One God and one faith, but three persons, therefore also three articles or confessions. Let us briefly run over the words.

Article I.

I believe in God the Father Almighty, Maker of heaven and earth.

This portrays and sets forth most briefly what is the essence, will, activity, and work of God the Father. For since the Ten Commandments have taught that we are to have not more than one God, the question might be asked, What kind of a person is God? What does He do? How can we praise or portray and describe Him, that He may be known? Now, that is taught in this and in the following article, so that the Creed is nothing else than the answer and confession of Christians arranged with respect to the First Commandment. As if you were to ask a little child: My dear, what sort of a God have you? What do you know of Him? he could say: This is my God: first, the Father, who has created heaven and earth; besides this only One I regard nothing else as God; for there is no one else who could create heaven and earth.

But for the learned, and those who are somewhat advanced [have acquired some Scriptural knowledge], these three articles may all be expanded and divided into as many parts as there are words. But now for young scholars let it suffice to indicate the most necessary points, namely, as we have said, that this article refers to the Creation: that we emphasize the words: Creator of heaven and earth But what is the force of this, or what do you mean by these words: I believe in God the Father Almighty, Maker, etc.? Answer: This is what I mean and believe, that I am a creature of God; that is, that He has given and constantly preserves to me my body, soul, and life, members great and small, all my senses, reason, and understanding, and so on, food and drink, clothing and support, wife and children, domestics, house and home, etc. Besides, He causes all creatures to serve for the uses and necessities of life — sun, moon and stars in the firmament, day and night, air, fire, water, earth, and whatever it bears and produces, birds and fishes, beasts, grain, and all kinds of produce, and whatever else there is of bodily and temporal goods, good government, peace, security. Thus we learn from this article that none of us has of himself, nor can preserve, his life nor anything that is here enumerated or can be enumerated, however small and unimportant a thing it might be, for all is comprehended in the word Creator.

Moreover, we also confess that God the Father has not only given us all that we have and see before our eyes, but daily preserves and defends us against all evil and misfortune, averts all sorts of danger and calamity; and that He does all this out of pure love and goodness, without our merit, as a benevolent Father, who cares for us that no evil befall us. But to speak more of this belongs in the other two parts of this article, where we say: Father Almighty

Now, since: all that we possess, and, moreover, whatever, in addition, is in heaven and upon the earth, is daily given, preserved, and kept for us by God, it is readily inferred and concluded that it is our duty to love, praise, and thank Him for it without ceasing, and, in short, to serve Him with all these things as He demands and has enjoined in the Ten Commandments.

Here we could say much if we were to expatiate, how few there are that believe this article. For we all pass over it, hear it and say it, but neither see nor consider what the words teach us. For if we believed it with the heart, we would also act accordingly, and not stalk about proudly, act defiantly, and boast as though we had life, riches, power, and honor, etc., of ourselves, so that others must fear and serve us, as is the practise of the wretched, perverse world, which is drowned in blindness, and abuses all the good things and gifts of God only for its own pride, avarice, lust, and luxury, and never once regards God, so as to thank Him or acknowledge Him as Lord and Creator.

Therefore, this article ought to humble and terrify us all, if we believed it. For we sin daily with eyes, ears, hands, body and soul, money and possessions, and with everything we have, especially those who even fight against the Word of God. Yet Christians have this advantage, that they acknowledge themselves in duty bound to serve God for all these things, and to be obedient to Him [which the world knows not how to do].

We ought, therefore, daily to practise this article, impress it upon our mind, and to remember it in all that meets our eyes, and in all good that falls to our lot, and wherever we escape from calamity or danger, that it is God who gives and does all these things, that therein we sense and see His paternal heart and His transcendent love toward us. Thereby the heart would be warmed and kindled to be thankful, and to employ all such good things to the honor and praise of God.

Thus we have most briefly presented the meaning of this article, as much as is at first necessary for the most simple to learn, both as to what we have and receive from God, and what we owe in return, which is a most excellent knowledge, but a far greater treasure. For here we see how the Father has given Himself to us, together with all creatures, and has most richly provided for us in this life, besides that He has overwhelmed us with unspeakable, eternal treasures by His Son and the Holy Ghost, as we shall hear.

Article II.

And in Jesus Christ, His only Son, our Lord, who was conceived by the Holy Ghost, born of the Virgin Mary; suffered under Pontius Pilate, was crucified, dead, and buried; He descended into hell; the third day He rose again from the dead; He ascended into heaven, and sitteth on the right hand of God the Father Almighty; from thence He shall come to judge the quick and the dead.

Here we learn to know the Second Person of the Godhead, so that we see what we have from God over and above the temporal goods aforementioned; namely, how He has completely poured forth Himself and withheld nothing from us that He has not given us. Now, this article is very rich and broad; but in order to expound it also briefly and in a childlike way, we shall take up one word and sum up in that the entire article, namely (as we have said), that we may here learn how we have been redeemed; and we shall base this on these words: In Jesus Christ, our Lord.

If now you are asked, What do you believe in the Second Article of Jesus

Christ? answer briefly: I believe that Jesus Christ, true Son of God, has become my Lord. But what is it to become Lord? It is this, that He has redeemed me from sin, from the devil, from death, and all evil. For before I had no Lord nor King, but was captive under the power of the devil, condemned to death, enmeshed in sin and blindness.

For when we had been created by God the Father, and had received from Him all manner of good, the devil came and led us into disobedience, sin, death, and all evil, so that we fell under His wrath and displeasure and were doomed to eternal damnation, as we had merited and deserved. There was no counsel, help, or comfort until this only and eternal Son of God in His unfathomable goodness had compassion upon our misery and wretchedness, and came from heaven to help us. Those tyrants and jailers, then, are all expelled now, and in their place has come Jesus Christ, Lord of life, righteousness, every blessing, and salvation, and has delivered us poor lost men from the jaws of hell, has won us, made us free, and brought us again into the favor and grace of the Father, and has taken us as His own property under His shelter and protection, that He may govern us by His righteousness, wisdom, power, life, and blessedness.

Let this then, be the sum of this article that the little word Lord signifies simply as much as Redeemer, i.e., He who has brought us from Satan to God, from death to life, from sin to righteousness, and who preserves us in the same. But all the points which follow in order in this article serve no other end than to explain and express this redemption, how and whereby it was accomplished, that is, how much it cost Him, and what He spent and risked that He might win us and bring us under His dominion, namely, that He became man, conceived and born without [any stain of] sin, of the Holy Ghost and of the Virgin Mary, that He might overcome sin; moreover, that He suffered, died and was buried, that He might make satisfaction for me and pay what I owe, not with silver nor gold, but with His own precious blood. And all this, in order to become my Lord; for He did none of these for Himself, nor had He any need of it. And after that He rose again from the dead, swallowed up and devoured death, and finally ascended into heaven and assumed the government at the Father's right hand, so that the devil and all powers must be subject to Him and lie at His feet, until finally, at the last day, He will completely part and separate us from the wicked world, the devil, death, sin, etc.

But to explain all these single points separately belongs not to brief sermons for children, but rather to the ampler sermons that extend throughout the entire year, especially at those times which are appointed for the purpose of treating at length of each article — of the birth, sufferings, resurrection, ascension of Christ, etc.

Ay, the entire Gospel which we preach is based on this, that we properly understand this article as that upon which our salvation and all our happiness rest, and which is so rich and comprehensive that we never can learn it fully.

Article III.

I believe in the Holy Ghost; the holy Christian Church, the communion of saints; the forgiveness of sins; the resurrection of the body; and the life everlasting. Amen.

This article (as I have said) I cannot relate better than to Sanctification, that through the same the Holy Ghost, with His office, is declared and depicted, namely, that He makes holy. Therefore we must take our stand upon the word Holy Ghost, because it is so precise and comprehensive that we cannot find another. For there are, besides, many kinds of spirits mentioned in the Holy Scriptures, as, the spirit of man, heavenly spirits, and evil spirits. But the Spirit of God alone is called Holy Ghost, that is, He who has sanctified and still sanctifies us. For as the Father is called Creator, the Son Redeemer, so the Holy Ghost, from His work, must be called Sanctifier, or One that makes holy. But how is such sanctifying done? Answer: Just as the Son obtains dominion, whereby He wins us, through His birth, death, resurrection, etc., so also the Holy Ghost effects our sanctification by the following parts, namely, by the communion of saints or the Christian Church, the forgiveness of sins, the resurrection of the body, and the life everlasting; that is, He first leads us into His holy congregation, and places us in the bosom of the Church, whereby He preaches to us and brings us to Christ.

For neither you nor I could ever know anything of Christ, or believe on Him, and obtain Him for our Lord, unless it were offered to us and granted to our hearts by the Holy Ghost through the preaching of the Gospel. The work is done and accomplished; for Christ has acquired and gained the treasure for us by His suffering, death, resurrection, etc. But if the work remained concealed so that no one knew of it, then it would be in vain and lost. That this treasure, therefore, might not lie buried, but be appropriated and enjoyed, God has caused the Word to go forth and be proclaimed, in which He gives the Holy Ghost to bring this treasure home and appropriate it to us. Therefore sanctifying is nothing else than bringing us to Christ to receive this good, to which we could not attain of ourselves.

Learn, then, to understand this article most clearly. If you are asked: What do you mean by the words: I believe in the Holy Ghost? you can answer: I believe that the Holy Ghost makes me holy, as His name implies. But whereby does He accomplish this, or what are His method and means to this end? Answer: By the Christian Church, the forgiveness of sins, the resurrection of the body, and the life everlasting. For, in the first place, He has a peculiar congregation in the world, which is the mother that begets and bears every Christian through the Word of God, which He reveals and preaches, [and through which] He illumines and enkindles hearts, that they understand, accept it, cling to it, and persevere in it.

For where He does not cause it to be preached and made alive in the heart, so that it is understood, it is lost, as was the case under the Papacy, where faith was entirely put under the bench, and no one recognized Christ as his Lord or the Holy Ghost as his Sanctifier, that is, no one believed that Christ is our Lord in the sense that He has acquired this treasure for us, without our works and merit, and made us acceptable to the Father. What, then, was lacking? This, that the Holy Ghost was not there to reveal it and cause it to be preached; but men and evil spirits were there, who taught us to obtain grace and be saved by our works. Therefore it is not a Christian Church either; for where Christ is not preached, there is no Holy Ghost who creates, calls, and gathers the Christian Church, without which no one can come to Christ the Lord. Let this suffice concerning the sum of this article. But because the parts which are here enumerated are not quite clear to the simple, we shall run over them also.

The Creed denominates the holy Christian Church, communionem sanctorum, a communion of saints; for both expressions, taken together, are identical. But formerly the one [the second] expression was not there, and it has been poorly and unintelligibly translated into German eine Gemeinschaft der Heiligen, a communion of saints. If it is to be rendered plainly, it must be expressed quite differently in the German idiom; for the word ecclesia properly means in German eine Versammlung, an assembly. But we are accustomed to the word church, by which the simple do not understand an assembled multitude, but the consecrated house or building, although the house ought not to be called a church, except only for the reason that the multitude assembles there. For we who assemble there make and choose for ourselves a particular place, and give a name to the house according to the assembly.

Thus the word Kirche (church) means really nothing else than a common assembly and is not German by idiom, but Greek (as is also the word ecclesia); for in their own language they call it kyria, as in Latin it is called curia. Therefore in genuine German, in our mother-tongue, it ought to be called a Christian congregation or assembly (eine christliche Gemeinde oder Sammlung), or, best of all and most clearly, holy Christendom (eine heilige Christenheit).

So also the word communio, which is added, ought not to be rendered communion (Gemeinschaft), but congregation (Gemeinde). And it is nothing else than an interpretation or explanation by which some one meant to explain what the Christian Church is. This our people, who understood neither Latin nor German, have rendered Gemeinschaft der Heiligen (communion of saints), although no German language speaks thus, nor understands it thus. But to speak correct German, it ought to be eine Gemeinde der Heiligen (a congregation of saints), that is, a congregation made up purely of saints, or, to speak yet more plainly, eine heilige Gemeinde, a holy congregation. I say this in order that the words Gemeinschaft der Heiligen (communion of saints) may be understood, because the expression has become so established by custom that it cannot well be eradicated, and it is treated almost as heresy if one should attempt to change a word.

But this is the meaning and substance of this addition: I believe that there is upon earth a little holy group and congregation of pure saints, under one head, even Christ, called together by the Holy Ghost in one faith, one mind, and understanding, with manifold gifts, yet agreeing in love, without sects or schisms. I am also a part and member of the same a sharer and joint owner of all the goods it possesses, brought to it and incorporated into it by the Holy Ghost by having heard and continuing to hear the Word of God, which is the beginning of entering it. For formerly, before we had attained to this, we were altogether of the devil, knowing nothing of God and of Christ. Thus, until the last day, the Holy Ghost abides with the holy congregation or Christendom, by means of which He fetches us to Christ and which He employs to teach and preach to us the Word, whereby He works and promotes sanctification, causing it [this community] daily to grow and become strong in the faith and its fruits which He produces.

We further believe that in this Christian Church we have forgiveness of sin, which is wrought through the holy Sacraments and Absolution, moreover, through all manner of consolatory promises of the entire Gospel. Therefore, whatever is to be preached concerning the Sacraments belongs here, and, in short, the whole Gospel and all the offices of Christianity, which also must be preached and taught without ceasing. For although the grace of God is secured through Christ, and sanctification is wrought by the Holy Ghost through the Word of God in the unity of the Christian Church, yet on account of our flesh which we bear about with us we are never without sin.

Everything, therefore, in the Christian Church is ordered to the end that we shall daily obtain there nothing but the forgiveness of sin through the Word and signs, to comfort and encourage our consciences as long as we live here. Thus, although we have sins, the [grace of the] Holy Ghost does not allow them to injure us, because we are in the Christian Church, where there is nothing but [continuous, uninterrupted] forgiveness of sin, both in that God forgives us, and in that we forgive, bear with, and help each other.

But outside of this Christian Church, where the Gospel is not, there is no forgiveness, as also there can be no holiness [sanctification]. Therefore all who seek and wish to merit holiness [sanctification], not through the Gospel and forgiveness of sin, but by their works, have expelled and severed themselves [from this Church].

Meanwhile, however, while sanctification has begun and is growing daily, we expect that our flesh will be destroyed and buried with all its uncleanness, and will come forth gloriously, and arise to entire and perfect holiness in a new eternal life. For now we are only half pure and holy, so that the Holy Ghost has ever [some reason why] to continue His work in us through the Word, and daily to dispense forgiveness, until we attain to that life where there will be no more forgiveness, but only perfectly pure and holy people, full of godliness and righteousness, removed and free from sin, death, and all evil, in a new, immortal, and glorified body.

Behold, all this is to be the office and work of the Holy Ghost, that He begin and daily increase holiness upon earth by means of these two things, the Christian Church and the forgiveness of sin. But in our dissolution He will accomplish it altogether in an instant, and will forever preserve us therein by the last two parts.

But the term Auferstehung des Fleisches (resurrection of the flesh) here employed is not according to good German idiom. For when we Germans hear the word Fleisch (flesh), we think no farther than of the shambles. But in good German idiom we would say Auferstehung des Leibes, or Leichnams (resurrection of the body). However, it is not a matter of much moment, if we only understand the words aright.

This, now, is the article which must ever be and remain in operation. For creation we have received; redemption, too, is finished. But the Holy Ghost carries on His work without ceasing to the last day. And for that purpose He has appointed a congregation upon earth by which He speaks and does everything. For He has not yet brought together all His Christian Church nor dispensed forgiveness. Therefore we believe in Him who through the Word daily brings us into the fellowship of this Christian Church, and through the same Word and the forgiveness of sins bestows, increases, and strengthens faith in order that when He has accomplished it all, and we abide therein, and die to the world and to all evil, He may finally make us perfectly and forever holy; which now we expect in faith through the Word.

Behold, here you have the entire divine essence, will, and work depicted most exquisitely in quite short and yet rich words wherein consists all our wisdom, which surpasses and exceeds the wisdom, mind, and reason of all men. For although the whole world with all diligence has endeavored to ascertain what God is, what He has in mind and does, yet has she never been able to attain to [the knowledge and understanding of] any of these things. But here we have everything in richest measure; for here in all three articles He has Himself revealed and opened the deepest abyss of his paternal heart and of His pure unutterable love. For He has created us for this very object, that He might redeem and sanctify us; and in addition to giving and imparting to us everything in heaven and upon earth, He has given to us even His Son and the Holy Ghost, by whom to bring us to Himself. For (as explained above) we could never attain to the knowledge of the grace and favor of the Father except through the Lord Christ, who is a mirror of the paternal heart, outside of whom we see nothing but an angry and terrible Judge. But of Christ we could know nothing either, unless it had been revealed by the Holy Ghost.

These articles of the Creed, therefore, divide and separate us Christians from all other people upon earth. For all outside of Christianity, whether heathen, Turks, Jews, or false Christians and hypocrites, although they believe in, and worship, only one true God, yet know not what His mind towards them is, and cannot expect any love or blessing from Him; therefore they abide in eternal wrath and damnation. For they have not the Lord Christ, and, besides, are not illumined and favored by any gifts of the Holy Ghost.

From this you perceive that the Creed is a doctrine quite different from the Ten Commandments; for the latter teaches indeed what we ought to do, but the former tells what God does for us and gives to us. Moreover, apart from this, the Ten Commandments are written in the hearts of all men; the Creed, however, no human wisdom can comprehend, but it must be taught by the Holy Ghost alone. The latter doctrine [of the Law], therefore makes no Christian, for the wrath and displeasure of God abide upon us still, because we cannot keep what God demands of us; but this [namely, the doctrine of faith] brings pure grace, and makes us godly and acceptable to God. For by this knowledge we obtain love and delight in all the commandments of God, because here we see that God gives Himself entire to us, with all that He has and is able to do, to aid and direct us in keeping the Ten Commandments — the Father, all creatures; the Son, His entire work; and the Holy Ghost, all His gifts.

Let this suffice concerning the Creed to lay a foundation for the simple, that they may not be burdened, so that, if they understand the substance of it, they themselves may afterwards strive to acquire more, and to refer to these parts whatever they learn in the Scriptures, and may ever grow and increase in richer understanding. For as long as we live here, we shall daily have enough to do to preach and to learn this.

Part Third. Of Prayer.

The Lord's Prayer.

We have now heard what we must do and believe, in which things the best and happiest life consists. Now follows the third part, how we ought to pray. For since we are so situated that no man can perfectly keep the Ten Commandments, even though he have begun to believe, and since the devil with all his power together with the world and our own flesh, resists our endeavors, nothing is so necessary as that we should continually resort to the ear of God, call upon Him, and pray to Him, that He would give, preserve, and increase in us faith and the fulfilment of the Ten Commandments, and that He would remove everything that is in our way and opposes us therein. But that we might know what and how to pray, our Lord Christ has Himself taught us both the mode and the words, as we shall see.

But before we explain the Lord's Prayer part by part, it is most necessary first to exhort and incite people to prayer, as Christ and the apostles also have done. And the first matter is to know that it is our duty to pray because of God's commandment. For thus we heard in the Second Commandment: Thou shalt not take the name of the lord, thy God, in vain, that we are there required to praise that holy name, and call upon it in every need, or to pray. For to call upon the name of God is nothing else than to pray. Prayer is therefore as strictly and earnestly commanded as all other commandments: to have no other God, not to kill, not to steal, etc. Let no one think that it is all the same whether he pray or not, as vulgar people do, who grope in such delusion and ask Why should I pray? Who knows whether God heeds or will hear my prayer? If I do not pray, some one else will. And thus they fall into the habit of never praying, and frame a pretext, as though we taught that there is no duty or need of prayer, because we reject false and hypocritical prayers.

But this is true indeed that such prayers as have been offered hitherto when men were babbling and bawling in the churches were no prayers. For such external matters, when they are properly observed, may be a good exercise for young children, scholars, and simple persons, and may be called singing or reading, but not really praying. But praying, as the Second Commandment teaches, is to call upon God in every need. This He requires of us, and has not left it to our choice. But it is our duty and obligation to pray if we would be Christians, as much as it is our duty and obligation to obey our parents and the government; for by calling upon it and praying the name of God is honored and profitably employed. This you must note above all things, that thereby you may silence and repel such thoughts as would keep and deter us from prayer. For just as it would be idle for a son to say to his father, "Of what advantage is my obedience? I will go and do what I can; it is all the same"; but there stands the commandment, Thou shalt and must do it, so also here it is not left to my will to do it or leave it undone, but prayer shall and must be offered at the risk of God's wrath and displeasure.

This is therefore to be understood and noted before everything else, in order that thereby we may silence and repel the thoughts which would keep and deter us from praying, as though it were not of much consequence if we do not pray, or as though it were commanded those who are holier and in better favor with God than we; as, indeed, the human heart is by nature so despondent that it always flees from God and imagines that He does not wish or desire our prayer, because we are sinners and have merited nothing but wrath. Against such thoughts (I say) we should regard this commandment and turn to God, that we may not by such disobedience excite His anger still more. For by this commandment He gives us plainly to understand that He will not cast us from Him nor chase us away, although we are sinners, but rather draw us to Himself, so that we might humble ourselves before Him, bewail this misery and plight of ours, and pray for grace and help. Therefore we read in the Scriptures that He is angry also with those who were smitten for their sin, because they did not return to Him and by their prayers assuage His wrath and seek His grace.

Now, from the fact that it is so solemnly commanded to pray, you are to conclude and think, that no one should by any means despise his prayer, but rather set great store by it, and always seek an illustration from the other commandments. A child should by no means despise his obedience to father and mother, but should always think: This work is a work of obedience, and what I do I do with no other intention than that I may walk in the obedience and commandment of God, on which I can settle and stand firm, and esteem it a great thing, not on account of my worthiness, but on account of the commandment. So here also, what and for what we pray we should regard as demanded by God and done in obedience to Him, and should reflect thus: On my account it would amount to nothing; but it shall avail, for the reason that God has commanded it. Therefore everybody, no matter what he has to say in prayer, should always come before God in obedience to this commandment.

We pray, therefore, and exhort every one most diligently to take this to heart and by no means to despise our prayer. For hitherto it has been taught thus in the devil's name that no one regarded these things, and men supposed it to be sufficient to have done the work, whether God would hear it or not. But that is staking prayer on a risk, and murmuring it at a venture, and therefore it is a lost prayer. For we allow such thoughts as these to lead us astray and deter us: I am not holy or worthy enough; if I were as godly and holy as St. Peter or St. Paul, then I would pray. But put such thoughts far away, for just the same commandment which applied to St. Paul applies also to me; and the Second Commandment is given as much on my account as on his account, so that he can boast of no better or holier commandment.

Therefore you should say: My prayer is as precious, holy, and pleasing to God as that of St. Paul or of the most holy saints. This is the reason: For I will gladly grant that he is holier in his person, but not on account of the commandment; since God does not regard prayer on account of the person, but on account of His word and obedience thereto. For on the commandment on which all the saints rest their prayer I, too, rest mine. Moreover I pray for the same thing for which they all pray and ever have prayed; besides, I have just as great a need of it as those great saints, yea, even a greater one than they.

Let this be the first and most important point, that all our prayers must be based and rest upon obedience to God, irrespective of our person, whether we be sinners or saints, worthy or unworthy. And we must know that God will not have it treated as a jest, but be angry, and punish all who do not pray, as surely as He punishes all other disobedience; next, that He will not suffer our prayers to be in vain or lost. For if He did not intend to answer your prayer, He would not bid you pray and add such a severe commandment to it.

In the second place, we should be the more urged and incited to pray because God has also added a promise, and declared that it shall surely be done to us as we pray, as He says Ps. 50, 15: Call upon Me in the day of trouble: I will deliver thee. And Christ in the Gospel of St. Matthew, 7, 7: Ask, and it shall be given you. For every one that asketh receiveth. Such promises ought certainly to encourage and kindle our hearts to pray with pleasure and delight, since He testifies with His [own] word that our prayer is heartily pleasing to Him, moreover, that it shall assuredly be heard and granted, in order that we may not despise it or think lightly of it, and pray at a venture.

This you can hold up to Him and say: Here I come, dear Father, and pray, not of my own purpose nor upon my own worthiness, but at Thy commandment and promise, which cannot fail or deceive me. Whoever, therefore, does not believe this promise must know again that he excites God to anger as a person who most highly dishonors Him and reproaches Him with falsehood.

Besides this, we should be incited and drawn to prayer because in addition to this commandment and promise God anticipates us, and Himself arranges the words and form of prayer for us, and places them upon our lips as to how and what we should pray, that we may see how heartily He pities us in our distress, and may never doubt that such prayer is pleasing to Him and shall certainly be answered; which [the Lord's Prayer] is a great advantage indeed over all other prayers that we might compose ourselves. For in them the conscience would ever be in doubt and say: I have prayed, but who knows how it pleases Him, or whether I have hit upon the right proportions and form? Hence there is no nobler prayer to be found upon earth than the Lord's Prayer which we daily pray because it has this excellent testimony, that God loves to hear it, which we ought not to surrender for all the riches of the world.

And it has been prescribed also for this reason that we should see and consider the distress which ought to urge and compel us to pray without ceasing. For whoever would pray must have something to present, state, and name which he desires; if not, it cannot be called a prayer.

Therefore we have rightly rejected the prayers of monks and priests, who howl and growl day and night like fiends; but none of them think of praying for a hair's breadth of anything. And if we would assemble all the churches, together with all ecclesiastics, they would be obliged to confess that they have never from the heart prayed for even a drop of wine. For none of them has ever purposed to pray from obedience to God and faith in His promise, nor has any one regarded any distress, but (when they had done their best) they thought no further than this, to do a good work, whereby they might repay God, as being unwilling to take anything from Him, but wishing only to give Him something.

But where there is to be a true prayer there must be earnestness. Men must feel their distress, and such distress as presses them and compels them to call and cry out then prayer will be made spontaneously, as it ought to be, and men will require no teaching how to prepare for it and to attain to the proper devotion. But the distress which ought to concern us most, both as regards ourselves and every one, you will find abundantly set forth in the Lord's Prayer. Therefore it is to serve also to remind us of the same, that we contemplate it and lay it to heart, lest we become remiss in prayer. For we all have enough that we lack, but the great want is that we do not feel nor see it. Therefore God also requires that you lament and plead such necessities and wants, not because He does not know them, but that you may kindle your heart to stronger and greater desires, and make wide and open your cloak to receive much.

Therefore, every one of us should accustom himself from his youth daily to pray for all his wants, whenever he is sensible of anything affecting his interests or that of other people among whom he may live, as for preachers, the government, neighbors, domestics, and always (as we have said) to hold up to God His commandment and promise, knowing that He will not have them disregarded. This I say because I would like to see these things brought home again to the people that they might learn to pray truly, and not go about coldly and indifferently, whereby they become daily more unfit for prayer; which is just what the devil desires, and for what he works with all his powers. For he is well aware what damage and harm it does him when prayer is in proper practise. For this we must know, that all our shelter and protection rest in prayer alone. For we are far too feeble to cope with the devil and all his power and adherents that set themselves against us, and they might easily crush us under their feet. Therefore we must consider and take up those weapons with which Christians must be armed in order to stand against the devil. For what do you think has hitherto accomplished such great things, has checked or quelled the counsels, purposes, murder, and riot of our enemies, whereby the devil thought to crush us, together with the Gospel, except that the prayer of a few godly men intervened like a wall of iron on our side? They should else have witnessed a far different tragedy, namely, how the devil would have destroyed all Germany in its own blood. But now they may confidently deride it and make a mock of it, however, we shall nevertheless be a match both for themselves and the devil by prayer alone, if we only persevere diligently and not become slack. For whenever a godly Christian prays: Dear Father let Thy will be done, God speaks from on high and says: Yes, dear child, it shall be so, in spite of the devil and all the world.

Let this be said as an exhortation, that men may learn, first of all, to esteem prayer as something great and precious, and to make a proper distinction between babbling and praying for something. For we by no means reject prayer, but the bare, useless howling and murmuring we reject, as Christ Himself also rejects and prohibits long palavers. Now we shall most briefly and clearly treat of the Lord's Prayer. Here there is comprehended in seven successive articles, or petitions, every need which never ceases to relate to us, and each so great that it ought to constrain us to keep praying it all our lives.

The First Petition.

Hallowed be Thy name.

This is, indeed, somewhat obscure, and not expressed in good German, for in our mother-tongue we would say: Heavenly Father, help that by all means Thy name may be holy. But what is it to pray that His name may be holy? Is it not holy already? Answer: Yes, it is always holy in its nature, but in our use it is not holy. For God's name was given us when we became Christians and were baptized, so that we are called children of God and have the Sacraments by which He so incorporates us in Himself that everything which is God's must serve for our use.

Here now the great need exists for which we ought to be most concerned, that this name have its proper honor, be esteemed holy and sublime as the greatest treasure and sanctuary that we have; and that as godly children we pray that the name of God, which is already holy in heaven, may also be and remain holy with us upon earth and in all the world.

But how does it become holy among us? Answer, as plainly as it can be said: When both our doctrine and life are godly and Christian. For since in this prayer we call God our Father, it is our duty always to deport and demean ourselves as godly children, that He may not receive shame, but honor and praise from us.

Now the name of God is profaned by us either in words or in works. (For whatever we do upon the earth must be either words or works, speech or act.) In the first place, then, it is profaned when men preach, teach, and speak in the name of God what is false and misleading, so that His name must serve to adorn and to find a market for falsehood. That is, indeed, the greatest profanation and dishonor of the divine name. Furthermore, also when men, by swearing, cursing, conjuring, etc., grossly abuse the holy name as a cloak for their shame. In the second place also by an openly wicked life and works, when those who are called Christians and the people of God are adulterers, drunkards, misers, envious, and slanderers. Here again must the name of God come to shame and be profaned because of us. For just as it is a shame and disgrace to a natural father to have a bad perverse child that opposes him in words and deeds, so that on its account he suffers contempt and reproach, so also it brings dishonor upon God if we who are called by His name and have all manner of goods from Him teach, speak, and live in any other manner except as godly and heavenly children, so that people say of us that we must be not God's, but the devil's children.

Thus you see that in this petition we pray just for that which God demands in the Second Commandment; namely, that His name be not taken in vain to swear, curse, lie, deceive, etc., but be usefully employed to the praise and honor of God. For whoever employs the name of God for any sort of wrong profanes and desecrates this holy name, as aforetime a church was considered desecrated when a murder or any other crime had been committed in it, or when a pyx or relic was desecrated, as being holy in themselves, yet become unholy in use. Thus this point is easy and clear if only the language is understood, that to hallow is the same as in our idiom to praise, magnify, and honor both in word and deed.

Here, now, learn how great need there is of such prayer. For because we see how full the world is of sects and false teachers, who all wear the holy name as a cover and sham for their doctrines of devils, we ought by all means to pray without ceasing, and to cry and call upon God against all such as preach and believe falsely and whatever opposes and persecutes our Gospel and pure doctrine, and would suppress it, as bishops, tyrants, enthusiasts, etc. Likewise also for ourselves who have the Word of God, but are not thankful for it, nor live as we ought according to the same. If now you pray for this with your heart, you can be sure that it pleases God; for He will not hear anything more dear to Him than that His honor and praise is exalted above everything else, and His Word is taught in its purity and is esteemed precious and dear.

The Second Petition.

Thy kingdom come.

As we prayed in the First Petition concerning the honor and name of God that He would prevent the world from adorning its lies and wickedness with it, but cause it to be esteemed sublime and holy both in doctrine and life, so that He may be praised and magnified in us, so here we pray that His kingdom also may come. But just as the name of God is in itself holy, and we pray nevertheless that it be holy among us, so also His kingdom comes of itself, without our prayer, yet we pray nevertheless that it may come to us, that is, prevail among us and with us, so that we may be a part of those among whom His name is hallowed and His kingdom prospers.

But what is the kingdom of God? Answer: Nothing else than what we learned in the Creed, that God sent His Son Jesus Christ our Lord, into the world to redeem and deliver us from the power of the devil, and to bring us to Himself, and to govern us as a King of righteousness, life and salvation against sin death, and an evil conscience, for which end He has also bestowed His Holy Ghost, who is to bring these things home to us by His holy Word, and to illumine and strengthen us in the faith by His power.

Therefore we pray here in the first place that this may become effective with us, and that His name be so praised through the holy Word of God and a Christian life that both we who have accepted it may abide and daily grow therein, and that it may gain approbation and adherence among other people and proceed with power throughout the world, that many may find entrance into the Kingdom of Grace, be made partakers of redemption, being led thereto by the Holy Ghost, in order that thus we may all together remain forever in the one kingdom now begun.

For the coming of God's Kingdom to us occurs in two ways; first, here in time through the Word and faith; and secondly, in eternity forever through revelation. Now we pray for both these things, that it may come to those who are not yet in it, and, by daily increase, to us who have received the same, and hereafter in eternal life. All this is nothing else than saying: Dear Father, we pray, give us first Thy Word, that the Gospel be preached properly throughout the world; and secondly, that it be received in faith, and work and live in us, so that through the Word and the power of the Holy Ghost Thy kingdom may prevail among us, and the kingdom of the devil be put down, that he may have no right or power over us, until at last it shall be utterly destroyed, and sin, death, and hell shall be exterminated, that we may live forever in perfect righteousness and blessedness.

From this you perceive that we pray here not for a crust of bread or a temporal, perishable good, but for an eternal inestimable treasure and everything that God Himself possesses; which is far too great for any human heart to think of desiring if He had not Himself commanded us to pray for the same. But because He is God, He also claims the honor of giving much more and more abundantly than any one can comprehend, — like an eternal, unfailing fountain, which, the more it pours forth and overflows, the more it continues to give, — and He desires nothing more earnestly of us than that we ask much and great things of Him, and again is angry if we do not ask and pray confidently.

For just as when the richest and most mighty emperor would bid a poor beggar ask whatever he might desire, and were ready to give great imperial presents, and the fool would beg only for a dish of gruel, he would be rightly considered a rogue and a scoundrel who treated the command of his imperial majesty as a jest and sport, and was not worthy of coming into his presence: so also it is a great reproach and dishonor to God if we, to whom He offers and pledges so many unspeakable treasures, despise the same, or have not the confidence to receive them, but scarcely venture to pray for a piece of bread.

All this is the fault of the shameful unbelief which does not look to God for as much good as will satisfy the stomach, much less expects without doubt such eternal treasures of God. Therefore we must strengthen ourselves against it, and let this be our first prayer; then, indeed, we shall have all else in abundance, as Christ teaches [Matt. 6, 33]: Seek ye first the kingdom of God and His righteousness and all these things shall be added unto you. For how could He allow us to suffer want and to be straitened in temporal things when He promises that which is eternal and imperishable?

The Third Petition.

Thy will be done on earth as it is in heaven.

Thus far we have prayed that God's name be honored by us, and that His kingdom prevail among us; in which two points is comprehended all that pertains to the honor of God and to our salvation, that we receive as our own God and all His riches. But now a need just as great arises, namely, that we firmly keep them, and do not suffer ourselves to be torn therefrom. For as in a good government it is not only necessary that there be those who build and govern well, but also those who make defense, afford protection and maintain it firmly, so here likewise, although we have prayed for the greatest need, for the Gospel, faith, and the Holy Ghost, that He may govern us and redeem us from the power of the devil, we must also pray that His will be done. For there will be happenings quite strange if we are to abide therein, as we shall have to suffer many thrusts and blows on that account from everything that ventures to oppose and prevent the fulfilment of the two petitions that precede.

For no one believes how the devil opposes and resists them, and cannot suffer that any one teach or believe aright. And it hurts him beyond measure to suffer his lies and abominations, that have been honored under the most specious pretexts of the divine name, to be exposed, and to be disgraced himself, and, besides, be driven out of the heart, and suffer such a breach to be made in his kingdom. Therefore he chafes and rages as a fierce enemy with all his power and might, and marshals all his subjects, and, in addition enlists the world and our own flesh as his allies. For our flesh is in itself indolent and inclined to evil, even though we have accepted and believe the Word of God. The world, however, is perverse and wicked; this he incites against us, fans and stirs the fire, that he may hinder and drive us back, cause us to fall, and again bring us under his power. Such is all his will, mind, and thought, for which he strives day and night, and never rests a moment, employing all arts, wiles, ways, and means whichever he can invent.

If we would be Christians, therefore, we must surely expect and reckon upon having the devil with all his angels and the world as our enemies, who will bring every possible misfortune and grief upon us. For where the Word of God is preached, accepted, or believed, and produces fruit, there the holy cross cannot be wanting. And let no one think that he shall have peace; but he must risk what whatever he has upon earth — possessions, honor. house and estate, wife and children, body and life. Now, this hurts our flesh and the old Adam; for the test is to be steadfast and to suffer with patience in whatever way we are assailed, and to let go whatever is taken from us.

Hence there is just as great need, as in all the others, that we pray without ceasing: "Dear Father, Thy will be done, not the will of the devil and of our enemies, nor of anything that would persecute and suppress Thy holy Word or hinder Thy kingdom; and grant that we may bear with patience and overcome whatever is to be endured on that account, lest our poor flesh yield or fall away from weakness or sluggishness."

Behold, thus we have in these three petitions, in the simplest manner, the need which relates to God Himself, yet all for our sakes. For whatever we pray concerns only us, namely, as we have said, that what must be done anyway without us, may also be done in us. For as His name must be hallowed and His kingdom come without our prayer, so also His will must be done and succeed although the devil with all his adherents raise a great tumult, are angry and rage against it, and undertake to exterminate the Gospel utterly. But for our own sakes we must pray that even against their fury His will be done without hindrance also among us, that they may not be able to accomplish anything and we remain firm against all violence and persecution, and submit to such will of God.

Such prayer, then, is to be our protection and defense now, is to repel and put down all that the devil, Pope, bishops, tyrants, and heretics can do against our Gospel. Let them all rage and attempt their utmost, and deliberate and resolve how they may suppress and exterminate us, that their will and counsel may prevail: over and against this one or two Christians with this petition alone shall be our wall against which they shall run and dash themselves to pieces. This consolation and confidence we have, that the will and purpose of the devil and of all our enemies shall and must fail and come to naught, however proud, secure, and powerful they know themselves to be. For if their will were not broken and hindered, the kingdom of God could not abide on earth nor His name be hallowed.

The Fourth Petition.

Give us this day our daily bread.

Here, now, we consider the poor breadbasket, the necessaries of our body and of the temporal life. It is a brief and simple word, but it has a very wide scope. For when you mention and pray for daily bread, you pray for everything that is necessary in order to have and enjoy daily bread and, on the other hand, against everything which interferes with it. Therefore you must open wide and extend your thoughts not only to the oven or the flour-bin but to the distant field and the entire land, which bears and brings to us daily bread and every sort of sustenance. For if God did not cause it to grow, and bless and preserve it in the field, we could never take bread from the oven or have any to set upon the table.

To comprise it briefly, this petition includes everything that belongs to our entire life in the world, because on that account alone do we need daily bread. Now for our life it is not only necessary that our body have food and covering and other necessaries, but also that we spend our days in peace and quiet among the people with whom we live and have intercourse in daily business and conversation and all sorts of doings, in short, whatever pertains both to the domestic and to the neighborly or civil relation and government. For where these two things are hindered [intercepted and disturbed] that they do not prosper as they ought, the necessaries of life also are impeded, so that ultimately life cannot be maintained. And there is, indeed, the greatest need to pray for temporal authority and government, as that by which most of all God preserves to us our daily bread and all the comforts of this life. For though we have received of God all good things in abundance we are not able to retain any of them or use them in security and happiness, if He did not give us a permanent and peaceful government. For where there are dissension, strife, and war, there the daily bread is already taken away, or at least checked.

Therefore it would be very proper to place in the coat-of-arms of every pious prince a loaf of bread instead of a lion, or a wreath of rue, or to stamp it upon the coin, to remind both them and their subjects that by their office we have protection and peace, and that without them we could not eat and retain our daily bread. Therefore they are also worthy of all honor, that we give to them for their office what we ought and can, as to those through whom we enjoy in peace and quietness what we have, because otherwise we would not keep a farthing; and that, in addition, we also pray for them that through them God may bestow on us the more blessing and good.

Let this be a very brief explanation and sketch, showing how far this petition extends through all conditions on earth. Of this any one might indeed make a long prayer, and with many words enumerate all the things that are included therein, as that we pray God to give us food and drink, clothing, house, and home, and health of body; also that He cause the grain and fruits of the field to grow and mature well; furthermore, that He help us at home towards good housekeeping, that He give and preserve to us a godly wife, children, and servants, that He cause our work, trade, or whatever we are engaged in to prosper and succeed, favor us with faithful neighbors and good friends, etc. Likewise, that He give to emperors, kings, and all estates, and especially to the rulers of our country and to all counselors, magistrates, and officers, wisdom, strength, and success that they may govern well and vanquish the Turks and all enemies; to subjects and the common people, obedience, peace, and harmony in their life with one another, and on the other hand, that He would preserve us from all sorts of calamity to body and livelihood, as lightning, hail, fire, flood, poison, pestilence, cattle-plague, war and bloodshed, famine, destructive beasts, wicked men, etc. All this it is well to impress upon the simple, namely, that these things come from God, and must be prayed for by us.

But this petition is especially directed also against our chief enemy, the devil. For all his thought and desire is to deprive us of all that we have from God, or to hinder it; and he is not satisfied to obstruct and destroy spiritual government in leading souls astray by his lies and bringing them under his power, but he also prevents and hinders the stability of all government and honorable, peaceable relations on earth. There he causes so much contention, murder, sedition, and war also lightning and hail to destroy grain and cattle, to poison the air, etc. In short, he is sorry that any one has a morsel of bread from God and eats it in peace; and if it were in his power, and our prayer (next to God) did not prevent him, we would not keep a straw in the field, a farthing in the house, yea, not even our life for an hour, especially those who have the Word of God and would like to be Christians.

Behold, thus God wishes to indicate to us how He cares for us in all our need, and faithfully provides also for our temporal support. and although He abundantly grants and preserves these things even to the wicked and knaves, yet He wishes that we pray for them, in order that we may recognize that we receive them from His hand, and may feel His paternal goodness toward us therein. For when He withdraws His hand, nothing can prosper nor be maintained in the end, as, indeed, we daily see and experience. How much trouble there is now in the world only on account of bad coin, yea, on account of daily oppression and raising of prices in common trade, bargaining and labor on the part of those who wantonly oppress the poor and deprive them of their daily bread! This we must suffer indeed; but let them take care that they do not lose the common intercession, and beware lest this petition in the Lord's Prayer be against them.

The Fifth Petition.

And forgive us our trespasses, as we forgive those who trespass against us.

This part now relates to our poor miserable life, which, although we have and believe the Word of God, and do and submit to His will, and are supported by His gifts and blessings is nevertheless not without sin. For we still stumble daily and transgress because we live in the world among men who do us much harm and give us cause for impatience, anger, revenge, etc. Besides, we have Satan at our back, who sets upon us on every side, and fights (as we have heard) against all the foregoing petitions, so that it is not possible always to stand firm in such a persistent conflict.

Therefore there is here again great need to call upon God and to pray: Dear Father, forgive us our trespasses. Not as though He did not forgive sin without and even before our prayer (for He has given us the Gospel, in which is pure forgiveness before we prayed or ever thought about it). But this is to the intent that we may recognize and accept such forgiveness. For since the flesh in which we daily live is of such a nature that it neither trusts nor believes God, and is ever active in evil lusts and devices, so that we sin daily in word and deed, by commission and omission by which the conscience is thrown into unrest, so that it is afraid of the wrath and displeasure of God, and thus loses the comfort and confidence derived from the Gospel; therefore it is ceaselessly necessary that we run hither and obtain consolation to comfort the conscience again.

But this should serve God's purpose of breaking our pride and keeping us humble. For in case any one should boast of his godliness and despise others, God has reserved this prerogative to Himself, that the person is to consider himself and place this prayer before his eyes, and he will find that he is no better than others, and that in the presence of God all must lower their plumes, and be glad that they can attain forgiveness. And let no one think that as long as we live here he can reach such a position that he will not need such forgiveness. In short, if God does not forgive without ceasing, we are lost.

It is therefore the intent of this petition that God would not regard our sins and hold up to us what we daily deserve, but would deal graciously with us, and forgive, as He has promised, and thus grant us a joyful and confident conscience to stand before Him in prayer. For where the heart is not in right relation towards God, nor can take such confidence, it will nevermore venture to pray. But such a confident and joyful heart can spring from nothing else than the [certain] knowledge of the forgiveness of sin.

But there is here attached a necessary, yet consolatory addition: As we forgive. He has promised that we shall be sure that everything is forgiven and pardoned, yet in the manner that we also forgive our neighbor. For just as we daily sin much against God and yet He forgives everything through grace, so we, too, must ever forgive our neighbor who does us injury, violence, and wrong, shows malice toward us, etc. If, therefore you do not forgive, then do not think that God forgives you; but if you forgive, you have this consolation and assurance, that you are forgiven in heaven, not on account of your forgiving, — for God forgives freely and without condition, out of pure grace, because He has so promised, as the Gospel teaches, — but in order that He may set this up for our confirmation and assurance for a sign alongside of the promise which accords with this prayer, Luke 6, 37: Forgive, and ye shall be forgiven. Therefore Christ also repeats it soon after the Lord's Prayer, and says, Matt. 6,14: For if ye forgive men their trespasses, your heavenly Father will also forgive you, etc.

This sign is therefore attached to this petition, that, when we pray, we remember the promise and reflect thus: Dear Father, for this reason I come and pray Thee to forgive me, not that I can make satisfaction, or can merit anything by my works, but because Thou hast promised and attached the seal thereto that I should be as sure as though I had absolution pronounced by Thyself. For as much as Baptism and the Lord's Supper appointed as external signs, effect, so much also this sign can effect to confirm our consciences and cause them to rejoice. And it is especially given for this purpose, that we might use and practise it every hour, as a thing that we have with us at all times.

The Sixth Petition.

And lead us not into temptation.

We have now heard enough what toil and labor is required to retain all that for which we pray, and to persevere therein, which, however, is not achieved without infirmities and stumbling. Besides, although we have received forgiveness and a good conscience and are entirely acquitted, yet is our life of such a nature that one stands to-day and to-morrow falls. Therefore, even though we be godly now and stand before God with a good conscience, we must pray again that He would not suffer us to relapse and yield to trials and temptations.

Temptation, however, or (as our Saxons in olden times used to call it) Bekoerunge, is of three kinds, namely, of the flesh, of the world and of the devil. For in the flesh we dwell and carry the old Adam about our neck, who exerts himself and incites us daily to inchastity, laziness, gluttony and drunkenness, avarice and deception, to defraud our neighbor and to overcharge him, and, in short, to all manner of evil lusts which cleave to us by nature, and to which we are incited by the society, example and what we hear and see of other people, which often wound and inflame even an innocent heart.

Next comes the world, which offends us in word and deed, and impels us to anger and impatience. In short, there is nothing but hatred and envy, enmity, violence and wrong, unfaithfulness, vengeance, cursing, raillery slander, pride and haughtiness, with superfluous finery, honor, fame, and power, where no one is willing to be the least, but every one desires to sit at the head and to be seen before all.

Then comes the devil, inciting and provoking in all directions, but especially agitating matters that concern the conscience and spiritual affairs, namely, to induce us to despise and disregard both the Word and works of God to tear us away from faith, hope, and love and bring us into misbelief, false security, and obduracy, or, on the other hand, to despair, denial of God, blasphemy, and innumerable other shocking things. These are indeed snares and nets, yea, real fiery darts which are shot most venomously into the heart, not by flesh and blood, but by the devil.

Great and grievous, indeed, are these dangers and temptations which every Christian must bear, even though each one were alone by himself, so that every hour that we are in this vile life where we are attacked on all sides, chased and hunted down, we are moved to cry out and to pray that God would not suffer us to become weary and faint and to relapse into sin, shame, and unbelief. For otherwise it is impossible to overcome even the least temptation.

This, then, is leading us not into temptation, to wit, when He gives us power and strength to resist, the temptation, however, not being taken away or removed. For while we live in the flesh and have the devil about us, no one can escape temptation and allurements; and it cannot be otherwise than that we must endure trials, yea, be engulfed in them; but we pray for this, that we may not fall and be drowned in them.

To feel temptation is therefore a far different thing from consenting or yielding to it. We must all feel it, although not all in the same manner, but some in a greater degree and more severely than others; as, the young suffer especially from the flesh, afterwards, they that attain to middle life and old age, from the world, but others who are occupied with spiritual matters, that is, strong Christians, from the devil. But such feeling, as long as it is against our will and we would rather be rid of it, can harm no one. For if we did not feel it, it could not be called a temptation. But to consent thereto is when we give it the reins and do not resist or pray against it.

Therefore we Christians must be armed and daily expect to be incessantly attacked, in order that no one may go on in security and heedlessly, as though the devil were far from us, but at all times expect and parry his blows. For though I am now chaste, patient, kind, and in firm faith, the devil will this very hour send such an arrow into my heart that I can scarcely stand. For he is an enemy that never desists nor becomes tired, so that when one temptation ceases, there always arise others and fresh ones.

Accordingly, there is no help or comfort except to run hither and to take hold of the Lord's Prayer, and thus speak to God from the heart: Dear Father, Thou hast bidden me pray; let me not relapse because of temptations. Then you will see that they must desist, and finally acknowledge themselves conquered. Else if you venture to help yourself by your own thoughts and counsel, you will only make the matter worse and give the devil more space. For he has a serpent's head, which if it gain an opening into which he can slip, the whole body will follow without check. But prayer can prevent him and drive him back.

The Seventh and Last Petition.

But deliver us from evil. Amen.

In the Greek text this petition reads thus: Deliver or preserve us from the Evil One, or the Malicious One; and it looks as if He were speaking of the devil, as though He would comprehend everything in one so that the entire substance of all our prayer is directed against our chief enemy. For it is he who hinders among us everything that we pray for: the name or honor of God, God's kingdom and will, our daily bread, a cheerful good conscience, etc.

Therefore we finally sum it all up and say: Dear Father pray, help that we be rid of all these calamities. But there is nevertheless also included whatever evil may happen to us under the devil's kingdom — poverty, shame, death, and, in short, all the agonizing misery and heartache of which there is such an unnumbered multitude on the earth. For since the devil is not only a liar, but also a murderer, he constantly seeks our life, and wreaks his anger whenever he can afflict our bodies with misfortune and harm. Hence it comes that he often breaks men's necks or drives them to insanity, drowns some, and incites many to commit suicide, and to many other terrible calamities. Therefore there is nothing for us to do upon earth but to pray against this arch enemy without ceasing. For unless God preserved us, we would not be safe from him even for an hour.

Hence you see again how God wishes us to pray to Him also for all the things which affect our bodily interests, so that we seek and expect help nowhere else except in Him. But this matter He has put last; for if we are to be preserved and delivered from all evil, the name of God must first be hallowed in us, His kingdom must be with us, and His will be done. After that He will finally preserve us from sin and shame, and, besides, from everything that may hurt or injure us.

Thus God has briefly placed before us all the distress which may ever come upon us, so that we might have no excuse whatever for not praying. But all depends upon this, that we learn also to say Amen, that is, that we do not doubt that our prayer is surely heard and [what we pray] shall be done. For this is nothing else than the word of undoubting faith, which does not pray at a venture, but knows that God does not lie to him, since He has promised to grant it. Therefore, where there is no such faith, there cannot be true prayer either.

It is, therefore, a pernicious delusion of those who pray in such a manner that they dare not from the heart say yea and positively conclude that God hears them, but remain in doubt and say, How should I be so bold as to boast that God hears my prayer? For I am but a poor sinner, etc.

The reason for this is, they regard not the promise of God, but their own work and worthiness, whereby they despise God and reproach Him with lying, and therefore they receive nothing. As St. James says [1, 6]: But let him ask in faith, nothing wavering; for he that wavereth is like a wave of the sea, driven with the wind and tossed. For let not that man think that he shall receive anything of the Lord. Behold, such importance God attaches to the fact that we are sure we do not pray in vain, and that we do not in any way despise our prayer.

Part Fourth.

Of Baptism.

We have now finished the three chief parts of the common Christian doctrine. Besides these we have yet to speak of our two Sacraments instituted by Christ, of which also every Christian ought to have at least an ordinary, brief instruction, because without them there can be no Christian; although, alas! hitherto no instruction concerning them has been given. But, in the first place, we take up Baptism, by which we are first received into the Christian Church. However, in order that it may be readily understood we will treat of it in an orderly manner, and keep only to that which it is necessary for us to know. For how it is to be maintained and defended against heretics and sects we will commend to the learned.

In the first place, we must above all things know well the words upon which Baptism is founded, and to which everything refers that is to be said on the subject, namely, where the Lord Christ speaks in the last chapter of Matthew, v. 19:

Go ye therefore and teach all nations, baptizing them in the name of the Father, and of the Son, and of the Holy Ghost.

Likewise in St. Mark, the last chapter, v. 16:

He that believeth and is baptized shall be saved; but he that believeth not shall be damned .

In these words you must note, in the first place, that here stand God's commandment and institution, lest we doubt that Baptism is divine, not devised nor invented by men. For as truly as I can say, No man has spun the Ten Commandments, the Creed, and the Lord's Prayer out of his head, but they are revealed and given by God Himself, so also I can boast that Baptism is no human trifle, but instituted by God Himself, moreover, that it is most solemnly and strictly commanded that we must be baptized or we cannot be saved, lest any one regard it as a trifling matter, like putting on a new red coat. For it is of the greatest importance that we esteem Baptism excellent, glorious, and exalted, for which we contend and fight chiefly, because the world is now so full of sects clamoring that Baptism is an external thing, and that external things are of no benefit. But let it be ever so much an external thing here stand God's Word and command which institute, establish, and confirm Baptism. But what God institutes and commands cannot be a vain, but must be a most precious thing, though in appearance it were of less value than a straw. If hitherto people could consider it a great thing when the Pope with his letters and bulls dispensed indulgences and confirmed altars and churches, solely because of the letters and seals, we ought to esteem Baptism much more highly and more precious, because God has commanded it, and, besides, it is performed in His name. For these are the words, Go ye baptize; however, not in your name, but in the name of God.

For to be baptized in the name of God is to be baptized not by men, but by God Himself. Therefore although it is performed by human hands, it is nevertheless truly God's own work. From this fact every one may himself readily infer that it is a far higher work than any work performed by a man or a saint. For what work greater than the work of God can we do?

But here the devil is busy to delude us with false appearances, and lead us away from the work of God to our own works. For there is a much more splendid appearance when a Carthusian does many great and difficult works and we all think much more of that which we do and merit ourselves. But the Scriptures teach thus: Even though we collect in one mass the works of all the monks, however splendidly they may shine, they would not be as noble and good as if God should pick up a straw. Why? Because the person is nobler and better. Here, then, we must not estimate the person according to the works, but the works according to the person, from whom they must derive their nobility. But insane reason will not regard this, and because Baptism does not shine like the works which we do, it is to be esteemed as nothing.

From this now learn a proper understanding of the subject, and how to answer the question what Baptism is, namely thus, that it is not mere ordinary water, but water comprehended in God's Word and command, and sanctified thereby, so that it is nothing else than a divine water; not that the water in itself is nobler than other water, but that God's Word and command are added.

Therefore it is pure wickedness and blasphemy of the devil that now our new spirits, to mock at Baptism, omit from it God's Word and institution, and look upon it in no other way than as water which is taken from the well, and then blather and say: How is a handful of water to help the soul? Aye, my friend, who does not know that water is water if tearing things asunder is what we are after? But how dare you thus interfere with God's order, and tear away the most precious treasure with which God has connected and enclosed it, and which He will not have separated? For the kernel in the water is God's Word or command and the name of God which is a treasure greater and nobler than heaven and earth.

Comprehend the difference, then, that Baptism is quite another thing than all other water; not on account of the natural quality, but because something more noble is here added; for God Himself stakes His honor His power and might on it. Therefore it is not only natural water, but a divine, heavenly, holy, and blessed water, and in whatever other terms we can praise it, — all on account of the Word, which is a heavenly, holy Word, that no one can sufficiently extol, for it has, and is able to do, all that God is and can do [since it has all the virtue and power of God comprised in it]. Hence also it derives its essence as a Sacrament, as St. Augustine also taught: Aocedat verbum ad elementum et fit sacramentum. That is, when the Word is joined to the element or natural substance, it becomes a Sacrament, that is, a holy and divine matter and sign.

Therefore we always teach that the Sacraments and all external things which God ordains and institutes should not be regarded according to the coarse, external mask, as we regard the shell of a nut, but as the Word of God is included therein. For thus we also speak of the parental estate and of civil government. If we propose to regard them in as far as they have noses, eyes, skin, and hair flesh and bones, they look like Turks and heathen, and some one might start up and say: Why should I esteem them more than others? But because the commandment is added: Honor thy father and thy mother, I behold a different man, adorned and clothed with the majesty and glory of God. The commandment (I say) is the chain of gold about his neck, yea, the crown upon his head which shows to me how and why one must honor this flesh and blood.

Thus, and much more even, you must honor Baptism and esteem it glorious on account of the Word, since He Himself has honored it both by words and deeds; moreover, confirmed it with miracles from heaven. For do you think it was a jest that, when Christ was baptized, the heavens were opened and the Holy Ghost descended visibly, and everything was divine glory and majesty?

Therefore I exhort again that these two the water and the Word, by no means be separated from one another and parted. For if the Word is separated from it, the water is the same as that with which the servant cooks, and may indeed be called a bath-keeper's baptism. But when it is added, as God has ordained, it is a Sacrament, and is called Christ-baptism. Let this be the first part regarding the essence and dignity of the holy Sacrament.

In the second place, since we know now what Baptism is, and how it is to be regarded, we must also learn why and for what purpose it is instituted; that is, what it profits, gives and works. And this also we cannot discern better than from the words of Christ above quoted: He that believeth and is baptized shall be saved. Therefore state it most simply thus, that the power, work, profit, fruit, and end of Baptism is this, namely, to save. For no one is baptized in order that he may become a prince, but, as the words declare, that he be saved. But to be saved. we know. is nothing else than to be delivered from sin, death, and the devil, and to enter into the kingdom of Christ, and to live with Him forever.

Here you see again how highly and precious we should esteem Baptism, because in it we obtain such an unspeakable treasure, which also indicates sufficiently that it cannot be ordinary mere water. For mere water could not do such a thing, but the Word does it, and (as said above) the fact that the name of God is comprehended therein. But where the name of God is, there must be also life and salvation, that it may indeed be called a divine, blessed, fruitful, and gracious water; for by the Word such power is imparted to Baptism that it is a laver of regeneration, as St. Paul also calls it, Titus 3, 5.

But as our would-be wise, new spirits assert that faith alone saves, and that works and external things avail nothing, we answer: It is true, indeed, that nothing in us is of any avail but faith, as we shall hear still further. But these blind guides are unwilling to see this, namely, that faith must have something which it believes, that is, of which it takes hold, and upon which it stands and rests. Thus faith clings to the water, and believes that it is Baptism, in which there is pure salvation and life; not through the water (as we have sufficiently stated), but through the fact that it is embodied in the Word and institution of God, and the name of God inheres in it. Now, if I believe this, what else is it than believing in God as in Him who has given and planted His Word into this ordinance, and proposes to us this external thing wherein we may apprehend such a treasure?

Now, they are so mad as to separate faith and that to which faith clings and is bound though it be something external. Yea, it shall and must be something external, that it may be apprehended by the senses, and understood and thereby be brought into the heart, as indeed the entire Gospel is an external, verbal preaching. In short, what God does and works in us He proposes to work through such external ordinances. Wherever, therefore, He speaks, yea, in whichever direction or by whatever means He speaks, thither faith must look, and to that it must hold. Now here we have the words: He that believeth and is baptized shall be saved. To what else do they refer than to Baptism, that is, to the water comprehended in God's ordinance? Hence it follows that whoever rejects Baptism rejects the Word of God, faith, and Christ, who directs us thither and binds us to Baptism.

In the third place since we have learned the great benefit and power of Baptism, let us see further who is the person that receives what Baptism gives and profits. This is again most beautifully and clearly expressed in the words: He that believeth and is baptized shall be saved. That is, faith alone makes the person worthy to receive profitably the saving, divine water. For, since these blessings are here presented and promised in the words in and with the water, they cannot be received in any other way than by believing them with the heart. Without faith it profits nothing, notwithstanding it is in itself a divine superabundant treasure. Therefore this single word (He that believeth) effects this much that it excludes and repels all works which we can do, in the opinion that we obtain and merit salvation by them. For it is determined that whatever is not faith avails nothing nor receives anything.

But if they say, as they are accustomed: Still Baptism is itself a work, and you say works are of no avail for salvation; what then, becomes of faith? Answer: Yes, our works, indeed, avail nothing for salvation; Baptism, however, is not our work, but God's (for, as was stated, you must put Christ-baptism far away from a bath-keeper's baptism). God's works, however, are saving and necessary for salvation, and do not exclude, but demand, faith; for without faith they could not be apprehended. For by suffering the water to be poured upon you, you have not yet received Baptism in such a manner that it benefits you anything; but it becomes beneficial to you if you have yourself baptized with the thought that this is according to God's command and ordinance, and besides in God's name, in order that you may receive in the water the promised salvation. Now, this the fist cannot do, nor the body; but the heart must believe it.

Thus you see plainly that there is here no work done by us, but a treasure which He gives us, and which faith apprehends; just as the Lord Jesus Christ upon the cross is not a work, but a treasure comprehended in the Word, and offered to us and received by faith. Therefore they do us violence by exclaiming against us as though we preach against faith; while we alone insist upon it as being of such necessity that without it nothing can be received nor enjoyed.

Thus we have these three parts which it is necessary to know concerning this Sacrament especially that the ordinance of God is to be held in all honor, which alone would be sufficient, though it be an entirely external thing like the commandment, Honor thy father and thy mother, which refers to bodily flesh and blood. Therein we regard not the flesh and blood, but the commandment of God in which they are comprehended, and on account of which the flesh is called father and mother; so also, though we had no more than these words, Go ye and baptize, etc., it would be necessary for us to accept and do it as the ordinance of God. Now there is here not only God's commandment and injunction, but also the promise, on account of which it is still far more glorious than whatever else God has commanded and ordained, and is, in short, so full of consolation and grace that heaven and earth cannot comprehend it. But it requires skill to believe this, for the treasure is not wanting, but this is wanting that men apprehend it and hold it firmly.

Therefore every Christian has enough in Baptism to learn and to practise all his life; for he has always enough to do to believe firmly what it promises and brings: victory over death and the devil, forgiveness of sin, the grace of God, the entire Christ, and the Holy Ghost with His gifts. In short, it is so transcendent that if timid nature could realize it, it might well doubt whether it could be true. For consider, if there were somewhere a physician who understood the art of saving men from dying, or, even though they died, of restoring them speedily to life, so that they would thereafter live forever, how the world would pour in money like snow and rain, so that because of the throng of the rich no one could find access! But here in Baptism there is brought free to every one's door such a treasure and medicine as utterly destroys death and preserves all men alive.

Thus we must regard Baptism and make it profitable to ourselves, that when our sins and conscience oppress us, we strengthen ourselves and take comfort and say: Nevertheless I am baptized; but if I am baptized, it is promised me that I shall be saved and have eternal life, both in soul and body. For that is the reason why these two things are done in Baptism namely, that the body, which can apprehend nothing but the water, is sprinkled, and, in addition, the word is spoken for the soul to apprehend. Now, since both, the water and the Word, are one Baptism, therefore body and soul must be saved and live forever: the soul through the Word which it believes, but the body because it is united with the soul and also apprehends Baptism as it is able to apprehend it. We have, therefore, no greater jewel in body and soul, for by it we are made holy and are saved, which no other kind of life, no work upon earth, can attain.

Let this suffice respecting the nature, blessing, and use of Baptism, for it answers the present purpose.

Part Fifth.

Of the Sacrament of the Altar.

In the same manner as we have heard regarding Holy Baptism, we must speak also concerning the other Sacrament, namely, these three points: What is it? What are its benefits? and, Who is to receive it? And all these are established by the words by which Christ has instituted it, and which every one who desires to be a Christian and go to the Sacrament should know. For it is not our intention to admit to it and to administer it to those who know not what they seek, or why they come. The words, however, are these:

Our Lord Jesus Christ, the same night in which He was betrayed, took bread; and when He had given thanks, He brake it, and gave it to His disciples, and said, Take, eat; this is My body, which is given for you: this do in remembrance of Me.

After the same manner also He took the cup when He had supped, gave thanks, and gave it to them, saying, Drink ye all of it; this cup is the new testament in My blood, which is shed for you for the remission of sins: this do ye, as oft as ye drink it, in remembrance of Me.

Here also we do not wish to enter into controversy and contend with the traducers and blasphemers of this Sacrament, but to learn first (as we did regarding Baptism) what is of the greatest importance, namely that the chief point is the Word and ordinance or command of God. For it has not been invented nor introduced by any man, but without any one's counsel and deliberation it has been instituted by Christ. Therefore, just as the Ten Commandments, the Lord's Prayer, and the Creed retain their nature and worth although you never keep, pray, or believe them, so also does this venerable Sacrament remain undisturbed, so that nothing is detracted or taken from it, even though we employ and dispense it unworthily. What do you think God cares about what we do or believe, so that on that account He should suffer His ordinance to be changed? Why, in all worldly matters every thing remains as God has created and ordered it, no matter how we employ or use it. This must always be urged, for thereby the prating of nearly all the fanatical spirits can be repelled. For they regard the Sacraments, aside from the Word of God, as something that we do.

Now, what is the Sacrament of the Altar!

Answer: It is the true body and blood of our Lord Jesus Christ, in and under the bread and wine which we Christians are commanded by the Word of Christ to eat and to drink. And as we have said of Baptism that it is not simple water, so here also we say the Sacrament is bread and wine, but not mere bread and wine, such as are ordinarily served at the table, but bread and wine comprehended in, and connected with, the Word of God.

It is the Word (I say) which makes and distinguishes this Sacrament, so that it is not mere bread and wine, but is, and is called, the body and blood of Christ. For it is said: Accedat verbum ad elementum, et At sacramentum. If the Word be joined to the element it becomes a Sacrament. This saying of St. Augustine is so properly and so well put that he has scarcely said anything better. The Word must make a Sacrament of the element, else it remains a mere element. Now, it is not the word or ordinance of a prince or emperor, but of the sublime Majesty, at whose feet all creatures should fall, and affirm it is as He says, and accept it with all reverence fear, and humility.

With this Word you can strengthen your conscience and say: If a hundred thousand devils, together with all fanatics, should rush forward, crying, How can bread and wine be the body and blood of Christ? etc., I know that all spirits and scholars together are not as wise as is the Divine Majesty in His little finger. Now here stands the Word of Christ: Take, eat; this is My body; Drink ye all of it; this is the new testament in My blood, etc. Here we abide, and would like to see those who will constitute themselves His masters, and make it different from what He has spoken. It is true, indeed, that if you take away the Word or regard it without the words, you have nothing but mere bread and wine. But if the words remain with them as they shall and must, then, in virtue of the same, it is truly the body and blood of Christ. For as the lips of Christ say and speak, so it is, as He can never lie or deceive.

Hence it is easy to reply to all manner of questions about which men are troubled at the present time, such as this one: Whether even a wicked priest can minister at, and dispense, the Sacrament, and whatever other questions like this there may be. For here we conclude and say: Even though a knave takes or distributes the Sacrament, he receives the true Sacrament, that is, the true body and blood of Christ, just as truly as he who [receives or] administers it in the most worthy manner. For it is not founded upon the holiness of men, but upon the Word of God. And as no saint upon earth, yea, no angel in heaven, can make bread and wine to be the body and blood of Christ, so also can no one change or alter it, even though it be misused. For the Word by which it became a Sacrament and was instituted does not become false because of the person or his unbelief. For He does not say: If you believe or are worthy, you receive My body and blood, but: Take, eat and drink; this is By body and blood. Likewise: Do this (namely, what I now do, institute, give, and bid you take) . That is as much as to say, No matter whether you are worthy or unworthy, you have here His body and blood by virtue of these words which are added to the bread and wine. Only note and remember this well; for upon these words rest all our foundation, protection, and defense against all errors and deception that have ever come or may yet come.

Thus we have briefly the first point which relates to the essence of this Sacrament. Now examine further the efficacy and benefits on account of which really the Sacrament was instituted; which is also its most necessary part, that we may know what we should seek and obtain there. Now this is plain and clear from the words just mentioned: This is My body and blood, given and shed FOR YOU, for the remission of sins. Briefly that is as much as to say: For this reason we go to the Sacrament because there we receive such a treasure by and in which we obtain forgiveness of sins. Why so? Because the words stand here and give us this; for on this account He bids me eat and drink, that it may be my own and may benefit me, as a sure pledge and token, yea, the very same treasure that is appointed for me against my sins, death, and every calamity.

On this account it is indeed called a food of souls, which nourishes and strengthens the new man. For by Baptism we are first born anew; but (as we said before) there still remains, besides, the old vicious nature of flesh and blood in man, and there are so many hindrances and temptations of the devil and of the world that we often become weary and faint, and sometimes also stumble.

Therefore it is given for a daily pasture and sustenance, that faith may refresh and strengthen itself so as not to fall back in such a battle, but become ever stronger and stronger. For the new life must be so regulated that it continually increase and progress, but it must suffer much opposition. For the devil is such a furious enemy that when he sees that we oppose him and attack the old man, and that he cannot topple us over by force, he prowls and moves about on all sides, tries all devices, and does not desist until he finally wearies us, so that we either renounce our faith or yield hands and feet and become listless or impatient. Now to this end the consolation is here given when the heart feels that the burden is becoming too heavy, that it may here obtain new power and refreshment.

But here our wise spirits contort themselves with their great art and wisdom, crying out and bawling: How can bread and wine forgive sins or strengthen faith? Although they hear and know that we do not say this of bread and wine, because in itself bread is bread, but of such bread and wine as is the body and blood of Christ, and has the words attached to it. That, we say, is verily the treasure, and nothing else, through which such forgiveness is obtained. Now the only way in which it is conveyed and appropriated to us is in the words (Given and shed for you). For herein you have both truths, that it is the body and blood of Christ, and that it is yours as a treasure and gift. Now the body of Christ can never be an unfruitful, vain thing, that effects or profits nothing. Yet however great is the treasure in itself, it must be comprehended in the Word and administered to us, else we should never be able to know or seek it.

Therefore also it is vain talk when they say that the body and blood of Christ are not given and shed for us in the Lord's Supper, hence we could not have forgiveness of sins in the Sacrament. For although the work is accomplished and the forgiveness of sins acquired on the cross, yet it cannot come to us in any other way than through the Word. For what would we otherwise know about it, that such a thing was accomplished or was to be given us if it were not presented by preaching or the oral Word? Whence do they know of it, or how can they apprehend and appropriate to themselves the forgiveness, except they lay hold of and believe the Scriptures and the Gospel? But now the entire Gospel and the article of the Creed: I believe a holy Christian Church, the forgiveness of sin, etc., are by the Word embodied in this Sacrament and presented to us. Why, then, should we allow this treasure to be torn from the Sacrament when they must confess that these are the very words which we hear everywhere in the Gospel, and they cannot say that these words in the Sacrament are of no use, as little as they dare say that the entire Gospel or Word of God, apart from the Sacrament, is of no use?

Thus we have the entire Sacrament, both as to what it is in itself and as to what it brings and profits. Now we must also see who is the person that receives this power and benefit. That is answered briefly, as we said above of Baptism and often elsewhere: Whoever believes it has what the words declare and bring. For they are not spoken or proclaimed to stone and wood, but to those who hear them, to whom He says: Take and eat, etc. And because He offers and promises forgiveness of sin, it cannot be received otherwise than by faith. This faith He Himself demands in the Word when He says: Given and shed for you. As if He said: For this reason I give it, and bid you eat and drink, that you may claim it as yours and enjoy it. Whoever now accepts these words, and believes that what they declare is true, has it. But whoever does not believe it has nothing, as he allows it to be offered to him in vain, and refuses to enjoy such a saving good. The treasure, indeed, is opened and placed at every one's door, yea upon his table, but it is necessary that you also claim it, and confidently view it as the words suggest to you.

This, now, is the entire Christian preparation for receiving this Sacrament worthily. For since this treasure is entirely presented in the words, it cannot be apprehended and appropriated in any other way than with the heart. For such a gift and eternal treasure cannot be seized with the fist. Fasting and prayer, etc., may indeed be an external preparation and discipline for children, that the body may keep and bear itself modestly and reverently towards the body and blood of Christ; yet what is given in and with it the body cannot seize and appropriate. But this is done by the faith of the heart, which discerns this treasure and desires it. This may suffice for what is necessary as a general instruction respecting this Sacrament; for what is further to be said of it belongs to another time.

Conclusion

In conclusion, since we have now the true understanding and doctrine of the Sacrament, there is indeed need of some admonition and exhortation, that men may not let so great a treasure which is daily administered and distributed among Christians pass by unheeded, that is, that those who would be Christians make ready to receive this venerable Sacrament often. For we see that men seem weary and lazy with respect to it; and there is a great multitude of such as hear the Gospel, and, because the nonsense of the Pope has been abolished, and we are freed from his laws and coercion, go one, two, three years, or even longer without the Sacrament, as though they were such strong Christians that they have no need of it; and some allow themselves to be prevented and deterred by the pretense that we have taught that no one should approach it except those who feel hunger and thirst, which urge them to it. Some pretend that it is a matter of liberty and not necessary, and that it is sufficient to believe without it; and thus for the most part they go so far that they become quite brutish, and finally despise both the Sacrament and the Word of God.

Now, it is true, as we have said, that no one should by any means be coerced or compelled, lest we institute a new murdering of souls. Nevertheless, it must be known that such people as deprive themselves of, and withdraw from, the Sacrament so long a time are not to be considered Christians. For Christ has not instituted it to be treated as a show, but has commanded His Christians to eat and drink it, and thereby remember Him.

And, indeed, those who are true Christians and esteem the Sacrament precious and holy will urge and impel themselves unto it. Yet that the simple-minded and the weak who also would like to be Christians be the more incited to consider the cause and need which ought to impel them, we will treat somewhat of this point. For as in other matters pertaining to faith, love, and patience, it is not enough to teach and instruct only, but there is need also of daily exhortation, so here also there is need of continuing to preach that men may not become weary and disgusted, since we know and feel how the devil always opposes this and every Christian exercise, and drives and deters therefrom as much as he can.

And we have, in the first place, the clear text in the very words of Christ: Do this in remembrance of Me. These are bidding and commanding words by which all who would be Christians are enjoined to partake of this Sacrament. Therefore, whoever would be a disciple of Christ, with whom He here speaks, must also consider and observe this, not from compulsion, as being forced by men, but in obedience to the Lord Jesus Christ, and to please Him. However, if you say: But the words are added, As oft as ye do it; there He compels no one, but leaves it to our free choice, answer: That is true, yet it is not written that we should never do so. Yea, just because He speaks the words, As oft as ye do it, it is nevertheless implied that we should do it often; and it is added for the reason that He wishes to have the Sacrament free, not limited to special times, like the Passover of the Jews, which they were obliged to eat only once a year, and that just upon the fourteenth day of the first full moon in the evening, and which they must not vary a day. As if He would say by these words: I institute a Passover or Supper for you which you shall enjoy not only once a year, just upon this evening, but often, when and where you will, according to every one's opportunity and necessity, bound to no place or appointed time; although the Pope afterwards perverted it, and again made a Jewish feast of it.

Thus, you perceive, it is not left free in the sense that we may despise it. For that I call despising it if one allow so long a time to elapse and with nothing to hinder him yet never feels a desire for it. If you wish such liberty, you may just as well have the liberty to be no Christian, and neither have to believe nor pray; for the one is just as much the command of Christ as the other. But if you wish to be a Christian, you must from time to time render satisfaction and obedience to this commandment. For this commandment ought ever to move you to examine yourself and to think: See, what sort of a Christian I am! If I were one, I would certainly have some little longing for that which my Lord has commanded [me] to do.

And, indeed, since we act such strangers to it, it is easily seen what sort of Christians we were under the Papacy, namely, that we went from mere compulsion and fear of human commandments, without inclination and love, and never regarded the commandment of Christ. But we neither force nor compel any one; nor need any one do it to serve or please us. But this should induce and constrain you by itself, that He desires it and that it is pleasing to Him. You must not suffer men to coerce you unto faith or any good work. We are doing no more than to say and exhort you as to what you ought to do, not for our sake, but for your own sake. He invites and allures you; if you despise it, you must answer for it yourself.

Now, this is to be the first point, especially for those who are cold and indifferent, that they may reflect upon and rouse themselves. For this is certainly true, as I have found in my own experience, and as every one will find in his own case, that if a person thus withdraw from this Sacrament, he will daily become more and more callous and cold, and will at last disregard it altogether. To avoid this, we must, indeed, examine heart and conscience, and act like a person who desires to be right with God. Now, the more this is done, the more will the heart be warmed and enkindled, that it may not become entirely cold.

But if you say: How if I feel that I am not prepared? Answer: That is also my scruple, especially from the old way under the Pope, in which a person tortured himself to be so perfectly pure that God could not find the least blemish in us. On this account we became so timid that every one was instantly thrown into consternation and said to himself: Alas! you are unworthy! For then nature and reason begin to reckon our unworthiness in comparison with the great and precious good; and then it appears like a dark lantern in contrast with the bright sun, or as filth in comparison with precious stones. Because nature and reason see this, they refuse to approach and tarry until they are prepared so long that one week trails another, and one half year the other. But if you are to regard how good and pure you are, and labor to have no compunctions, you must never approach.

We must, therefore, make a distinction here among men. For those who are wanton and dissolute must be told to stay away; for they are not prepared to receive forgiveness of sin since they do not desire it and do not wish to be godly. But the others, who are not such callous and wicked people, and desire to be godly, must not absent themselves, even though otherwise they be feeble and full of infirmities, as St. Hilary also has said: If any one have not committed sin for which he can rightly be put out of the congregation and esteemed as no Christian, he ought not stay away from the Sacrament, lest he may deprive himself of life. For no one will make such progress that he will not retain many daily infirmities in flesh and blood.

Therefore such people must learn that it is the highest art to know that our Sacrament does not depend upon our worthiness. For we are not baptized because we are worthy and holy, nor do we go to confession because we are pure and without sin, but the contrary because we are poor miserable men and just because we are unworthy; unless it be some one who desires no grace and absolution nor intends to reform.

But whoever would gladly obtain grace and consolation should impel himself, and allow no one to frighten him away, but say: I, indeed, would like to be worthy, but I come, not upon any worthiness, but upon Thy Word, because Thou hast commanded it, as one who would gladly be Thy disciple, no matter what becomes of my worthiness. But this is difficult; for we always have this obstacle and hindrance to encounter, that we look more upon ourselves than upon the Word and lips of Christ. For nature desires so to act that it can stand and rest firmly on itself, otherwise it refuses to make the approach. Let this suffice concerning the first point.

In the second place, there is besides this command also a promise, as we heard above, which ought most strongly to incite and encourage us. For here stand the kind and precious words: This is My body, given for you. This is My blood, shed for you, for the remission of sins. These words, I have said, are not preached to wood and stone, but to me and you; else He might just as well be silent and not institute a Sacrament. Therefore consider, and put yourself into this YOU, that He may not speak to you in vain.

For here He offers to us the entire treasure which He has brought for us from heaven, and to which He invites us also in other places with the greatest kindness, as when He says in St. Matthew 11, 28: Come unto Me, all ye that labor and are heavy laden, and I will give you rest. Now it is surely a sin and a shame that He so cordially and faithfully summons and exhorts us to our highest and greatest good, and we act so distantly with regard to it, and permit so long a time to pass [without partaking of the Sacrament] that we grow quite cold and hardened, so that we have no inclination or love for it. We must never regard the Sacrament as something injurious from which we had better flee but as a pure wholesome, comforting remedy imparting salvation and comfort, which will cure you and give you life both in soul and body. For where the soul has recovered, the body also is relieved. Why, then, is it that we act as if it were a poison, the eating of which would bring death?

To be sure, it is true that those who despise it and live in an unchristian manner receive it to their hurt and damnation; for nothing shall be good or wholesome to them, just as with a sick person who from caprice eats and drinks what is forbidden him by the physician. But those who are sensible of their weakness, desire to be rid of it and long for help, should regard and use it only as a precious antidote against the poison which they have in them. For here in the Sacrament you are to receive from the lips of Christ forgiveness of sin which contains and brings with it the grace of God and the Spirit with all His gifts, protection, shelter, and power against death and the devil and all misfortune.

Thus you have, on the part of God, both the command and the promise of the Lord Jesus Christ. Besides this, on your part, your own distress which is about your neck, and because of which this command, invitation and promise are given, ought to impel you. For He Himself says: They that be whole need not a physician, but they that be sick; that is, those who are weary and heavy-laden with their sins, with the fear of death temptations of the flesh and of the devil. If therefore, you are heavy-laden and feel your weakness, then go joyfully to this Sacrament and obtain refreshment, consolation, and strength. For if you would wait until you are rid of such burdens, that you might come to the Sacrament pure and worthy, you must forever stay away. For in that case He pronounces sentence and says: If you are pure and godly, you have no need of Me, and I, in turn, none of thee. Therefore those alone are called unworthy who neither feel their infirmities nor wish to be considered sinners.

But if you say: What, then, shall I do if I cannot feel such distress or experience hunger and thirst for the Sacrament? Answer: For those who are so minded that they do not realize their condition I know no better counsel than that they put their hand into their bosom to ascertain whether they also have flesh and blood. And if you find that to be the case, then go, for your good, to St. Paul's Epistle to the Galatians, and hear what sort of a fruit your flesh is: Now the works of the flesh (he says [chap. 5, 19ff.]) are manifest, which are these: Adultery fornication uncleanness, lasciviousness, idolatry, witchcraft, hatred, variance, emulations, wrath, strife, seditions, heresies, envyings, murders, drunkenness, revelings, and such like.

Therefore, if you cannot feel it, at least believe the Scriptures, they will not lie to you and they know your flesh better than you yourself. Yea, St. Paul further concludes in Rom. 7, 18:1 know that in me, that is, in my flesh, dwelleth no good thing. If St. Paul may speak thus of his flesh, we do not propose to be better nor more holy. But that we do not feel it is so much the worse; for it is a sign that there is a leprous flesh which feels nothing, and yet [the leprosy] rages and keeps spreading. Yet as we have said, if you are quite dead to all sensibility, still believe the Scriptures, which pronounce sentence upon you. And, in short, the less you feel your sins and infirmities, the more reason have you to go to the Sacrament to seek help and a remedy.

In the second place, look about you and see whether you are also in the world, or if you do not know it, ask your neighbors about it. If you are in the world, do not think that there will be lack of sins and misery. For only begin to act as though you would be godly and adhere to the Gospel, and see whether no one will become your enemy, and, moreover, do you harm, wrong, and violence, and likewise give you cause for sin and vice. If you have not experienced it, then let the Scriptures tell you, which everywhere give this praise and testimony to the world.

Besides this, you will also have the devil about you, whom you will not entirely tread under foot, because our Lord Christ Himself could not entirely avoid him. Now, what is the devil? Nothing else than what the Scriptures call him, a liar and murderer. A liar, to lead the heart astray from the Word of God, and to blind it, that you cannot feel your distress or come to Christ. A murderer, who cannot bear to see you live one single hour. If you could see how many knives, darts, and arrows are every moment aimed at you, you would be glad to come to the Sacrament as often as possible. But there is no reason why we walk so securely and heedlessly, except that we neither think nor believe that we are in the flesh, and in this wicked world or in the kingdom of the devil.

Therefore, try this and practise it well, and do but examine yourself, or look about you a little, and only keep to the Scriptures. If even then you still feel nothing, you have so much the more misery to lament both to God and to your brother. Then take advice and have others pray for you, and do not desist until the stone be removed from your heart. Then, indeed, the distress will not fail to become manifest, and you will find that you have sunk twice as deep as any other poor sinner, and are much more in need of the Sacrament against the misery which unfortunately you do not see, so that, with the grace of God, you may feel it more and become the more hungry for the Sacrament, especially since the devil plies his force against you, and lies in wait for you without ceasing, to seize and destroy you, soul and body, so that you are not safe from him one hour. How soon can he have brought you suddenly into misery and distress when you least expect it!

Let this, then, be said for exhortation, not only for those of us who are old and grown, but also for the young people, who ought to be brought up in the Christian doctrine and understanding. For thereby the Ten Commandments, the Creed, and the Lord's Prayer might be the more easily inculcated to our youth, so that they would receive them with pleasure and earnestness, and thus would practise them from their youth and accustom themselves to them. For the old are now well-nigh done for, so that these and other things cannot be attained, unless we train the people who are to come after us and succeed us in our office and work, in order that they also may bring up their children successfully that the Word of God and the Christian Church may be preserved. Therefore let every father of a family know that it is his duty by the injunction and command of God, to teach these things to his children, or have them learn what they ought to know. For since they are baptized and received into the Christian Church, they should also enjoy this communion of the Sacrament, in order that they may serve us and be useful to us; for they must all indeed help us to believe, love, pray, and fight against the devil.

Selected Sermons of Martin Luther

Table of Contents

Christ's Holy Sufferings

The True and the False Views of Christ's Sufferings

Section I. the False Views of Christ's Sufferings.

1. In the first place, some reflect upon the sufferings of Christ in a way that they become angry at the Jews, sing and lament about poor Judas, and are then satisfied; just like by habit they complain of other persons, and condemn and spend their time with their enemies. Such an exercise may truly be called a meditation not on the sufferings of Christ, but on the wickedness of Judas and the Jews.

2. In the second place, others have pointed out the different benefits and fruits springing from a consideration of Christ's Passion. Here the saying ascribed to Albertus is misleading, that to think once superficially on the sufferings of Christ is better than to fast a whole year or to pray the Psalter every day, etc. The people thus blindly follow him and act contrary to the true fruits of Christ's Passion; for they seek therein their own selfish interests. Therefore they decorate themselves with pictures and booklets, with letters and crucifixes, and some go so far as to imagine that they thus protect themselves against the perils of water, of fire, and of the sword, and all other dangers. In this way the suffering of Christ is to work in them an absence of suffering, which is contrary to its nature and character.

3. A third class so, sympathize with Christ as to weep and lament for him because he was so innocent, like the women who followed Christ from Jerusalem, whom he rebuked, in that they should better weep for themselves and for their children. Such are they who run far away in the midst of the Passion season, and are greatly benefited by the departure of Christ from Bethany and by the pains and sorrows of the Virgin Mary, but they never get farther. Hence they postpone the Passion many hours, and God only knows whether it is devised more for sleeping than for watching. And among these fanatics are those who taught what great blessings come from the holy mass, and in their simple way they think it is enough if they attend mass. To this we are led through the sayings of certain teachers, that the mass opere operati, non opere operantis, is acceptable of itself, even without our merit and worthiness, just as if that were enough. Nevertheless the mass was not instituted for the sake of its own worthiness but to prove us, especially for the purpose of

meditating upon the sufferings of Christ. For where this is not done, we make a temporal, unfruitful work out of the mass, however good it may be in itself. For what help is it to you, that God is God, if he is not God to you? What benefit is it that eating and drinking are in themselves healthful and good, if they are not healthful for you, and there is fear that we never grow better by reason of our many masses, if we fail to seek the true fruit in them?

Section II. The True View of Christ's Sufferings.

4. Fourthly, they meditate on the Passion of Christ aright, who so view Christ that they become terror-stricken in heart at the sight, and their conscience at once sinks in despair. This terror-stricken feeling should spring forth, so that you see the severe wrath and the unchangeable earnestness of God in regard to sin and sinners, in that he was unwilling that his only and dearly beloved Son should set sinners free unless he paid the costly ransom for them as is mentioned in Is 53:8: "For the transgression of my people was he stricken." What happens to the sinner, when the dear child is thus stricken? An earnestness must be present that is inexpressible and unbearable, which a person so immeasurably great goes to meet, and suffers and dies for it; and if you reflect upon it real deeply, that God's Son, the eternal wisdom of the Father, himself suffers, you will indeed be terror-stricken; and the more you reflect the deeper will be the impression.

5. Fifthly, that you deeply believe and never doubt the least, that you are the one who thus martyred Christ. For your sins most surely did it. Thus St. Peter struck and terrified the Jews as with a thunderbolt in Acts 2:36-37, when he spoke to them all in common: "Him have ye crucified," so that three thousand were terror-stricken the same day and tremblingly cried to the apostles: "O beloved brethren what shall we do?" Therefore, when you view the nails piercing through his hands, firmly believe it is your work. Do you behold his crown of thorns, believe the thorns are your wicked thoughts, etc.

6. Sixthly, now see, where one thorn pierces Christ, there more than a thousand thorns should pierce thee, yea, eternally should they thus and even more painfully pierce thee. Where one nail is driven through his hands and feet, thou shouldest eternally suffer such and even more painful nails; as will be also visited upon those who, let Christ's sufferings be lost and fruitless as far as they are concerned. For this earnest mirror, Christ, will neither lie nor mock; whatever he says must be fully realized.

7. Seventhly, St. Bernard was so terror-stricken by Christ's sufferings that he said: I imagined I was secure and I knew nothing of the eternal judgment passed upon me in heaven, until I saw that the eternal Son of God took mercy upon me, stepped forward and offered himself on my behalf in the same judgment. Ah, it does not become me still to play and remain secure when such earnestness, is behind those sufferings. Hence he commanded the women: "Weep not for me, but weep for yourselves, and for your children." Lk. 23:28;

and gives in the 31st verse the reason: "For if they do these things in the green tree, what shall be done in the dry?" As if to say: Learn from my martyrdom what you have merited and how you should be rewarded. For here it is true that a little dog was slain in order to terrorize a big one. Likewise the prophet also said: "All generations shall lament and bewail themselves more than him"; it is not said they shall lament him, but themselves rather than him. Likewise were also the apostles terror-stricken in Acts 2:27, as mentioned before, so that they said to the apostles: "O, brethren, what shall we do?" So the church also sings: I will diligently meditate thereon, and thus my soul in me will exhaust itself.

8. Eighthly, one must skilfully exercise himself in this point, for the benefit of Christ's sufferings depends almost entirely upon man coming to a true knowledge of himself, and becoming terror-stricken and slain before himself. And where man does not come to this point, the sufferings of Christ have become of no true benefit to him. For the characteristic, natural work of Christ's sufferings is that they make all men equal and alike, so that as Christ was horribly martyred as to body and soul in our sins, we must also like him be martyred in our consciences by our sins. This does not take place by means of many words, but by means of deep thoughts and a profound realization of our sins. Take an illustration: If an evil-doer were judged because he had slain the child of a prince or king, and you were in safety, and sang and played, as if you were entirely innocent, until one seized you in a horrible manner and convinced you that you had enabled the wicked person to do the act; behold, then you would be in the greatest straits, especially if your conscience also revolted against you. Thus much more anxious you should be, when you consider Christ's sufferings. For the evil doers, the Jews, although they have now judged and banished God, they have still been the servants of your sins, and you are truly the one who strangled and crucified the Son of God through your sins, as has been said.

9. Ninthly, whoever perceives himself to be so hard and sterile that he is not terror-stricken by Christ's sufferings and led to a knowledge of him, he should fear and tremble. For it cannot be otherwise; you must become like the picture and sufferings of Christ, be it realized in life or in hell; you must at the time of death, if not sooner, fall into terror, tremble, quake and experience all Christ suffered on the cross. It is truly terrible to attend to this on your deathbed; therefore you should pray God to soften your heart and permit you fruitfully to meditate upon Christ's Passion. For it is impossible for us profoundly to meditate upon the sufferings of Christ of ourselves, unless God sink them into our hearts. Further, neither this meditation nor any other doctrine is given to you to the
end that you should fall fresh upon it of yourself, to accomplish the same; but you are first to seek and long for the grace of God, that you may accomplish it through God's grace and not through your own power. For in this way it

happens that those referred to above never treat the sufferings of Christ aright; for they never call upon God to that end, but devise out of their own ability their own way, and treat those sufferings entirely in a human and an unfruitful manner.

10 Tenthly, whoever meditates thus upon God's sufferings for a day, an hour, yea, for a quarter of an hour, we wish to say freely and publicly, that it is better than if he fasts a whole year, prays the Psalter every day, yea, than if he hears a hundred masses. For such a meditation changes a man's character and almost as in baptism he is born again, anew. Then Christ's suffering accomplishes its true, natural and noble work, it slays the old Adam, banishes all lust, pleasure and security that one may obtain from God's creatures; just like Christ was forsaken by all, even by God.

11. Eleventhly, since then such a work is not in our hands, it happens that sometimes we pray and do not receive it at the time; in spite of this one should not despair nor cease to pray. At times it comes when we are not praying for it, as God knows and wills; for it will be free and unbound: then man is distressed in conscience and is wickedly displeased with his own life, and it may easily happen that he does not know that Christ's Passion is working this very thing in him, of which perhaps he was not aware, just like the others so exclusively meditated on Christ's Passion that in their knowledge of self they could not extricate themselves out of that state of meditation. Among the first the sufferings of Christ are quite and true, among the others a show and false, and according to its nature God often turns the leaf, so that those who do not meditate on the Passion, really do, meditate on it; and those who bear the mass, do not hear it; and those who hear it not, do hear it.

Section III. The Comfort of Christ's Sufferings.

12. Until the present we have been in the Passion week and have celebrated Good Friday in the right way: now we come to Easter and Christ's resurrection. When man perceives his sins in this light and is completely terror-stricken in his conscience, he must be on his guard that his sins do not thus remain in his conscience, and nothing but pure doubt certainly come out of it; but just as the sins flowed out of Christ and we became conscious of them, so should we pour them again upon him and set our conscience free. Therefore see well to it that you act not like perverted people, who bite and devour themselves with their sins in their heart, and run here and there with their good works or their own satisfaction, or even work themselves out of this condition by means of indulgences and become rid of their sins; which is impossible, and, alas, such a false refuge of satisfaction and pilgrimages has spread far and wide.

13. Thirteenthly. Then cast your sins from yourself upon Christ, believe with a festive spirit that your sins are his wounds and sufferings, that he carries them and makes satisfaction for them, as Is 53:6 says: "Jehovah hath laid on him the iniquity of us all;" and St. Peter in his first Epistle 2:24: "Who his own

self bare our sins in his body upon the tree" of the cross; and St. Paul in 2 Cor. 5:21: "Him who knew no sin was made to be sin on our behalf; that we might become the righteousness of God in him." Upon these and like passages you must rely with all your weight, and so much the more the harder your conscience martyrs you. For if you do not take this course, but miss the opportunity of stilling your heart, then you will never secure peace, and must yet finally despair in doubt. For if we deal with our sins in our conscience and let them continue within us and be cherished in our hearts, they become much too strong for us to manage and they will live forever. But when we see that they are laid on Christ and he has triumphed over them by his resurrection and we fearlessly believe it, then they are dead and have become as nothing. For upon Christ they cannot rest, there they are swallowed up by his resurrection, and you see now no wound, no pain, in him, that is, no sign of sin. Thus St. Paul speaks in Rom. 4:25, that he was delivered up for our trespasses and was raised for our justification; that is, in his sufferings he made known our sins and also crucified them; but by his resurrection he makes us righteous and free from all sin, even if we believe the same differently.

14. Fourteenthly. Now if you are not able to believe, then, as I said before, you should pray to God for faith. For this is a matter in the hands of God that is entirely free, and is also bestowed alike at times knowingly, at times secretly, as was just said on the subject of suffering.

15. But now bestir yourself to the end: first, not to behold Christ's sufferings any longer; for they have already done their work and terrified you; but press through all difficulties and behold his friendly heart, how full of love it is toward you, which love constrained him to bear the heavy load of your conscience and your sin. Thus will your heart be loving and sweet toward him, and the assurance of your faith be strengthened. Then ascend higher through the heart of Christ to the heart of God, and see that Christ would not have been able to love you if God had not willed it in eternal love, to which Christ is obedient in his love toward you; there you will find the divine, good father heart, and, as Christ says, be thus drawn to the Father through Christ. Then will you understand the saying of Christ in Jn. 3:16: "God so loved the world that he gave his only begotten Son," etc. That means to know God aright, if we apprehend him not by his power and wisdom, which terrify us, but by his goodness and love; there our faith and confidence can then stand unmovable and man is truly thus born anew in God.

16. Sixteenthly. When your heart is thus established in Christ, and you are an enemy of sin, out of love and not out of fear of punishment, Christ's sufferings should also be an example for your whole life, and you should meditate on the same in a different way. For hitherto we have considered Christ's Passion as a sacrament that works in us and we suffer; now we consider it, that we also work, namely thus: if a day of sorrow or sickness weighs you down, think, how trifling that is, compared with the thorns and

nails of Christ. If you must do or leave undone what is distasteful to you: think, how Christ was led hither and thither, bound and a captive. Does pride attack you: behold, how your Lord was mocked and disgraced with murderers. Do unchastity and lust thrust themselves against you: think, how bitter it was for Christ to have his tender flesh torn, pierced and beaten again and again. Do hatred and envy war against you, or do you seek vengeance: remember how Christ with many tears and cries prayed for you and all his enemies, who indeed had more reason to seek revenge. If trouble or whatever adversity of body or soul afflict you, strengthen your heart and say: Ah, why then should I not also suffer a little since my Lord sweat blood in the garden because of anxiety and grief? That would be a lazy, disgraceful servant who would wish to lie in his bed while his lord was compelled to battle with the pangs of death.

17. Behold, one can thus find in Christ strength and comfort against all vice and bad habits. That is the right observance of Christ's Passion, and that is the fruit of his suffering, and he who exercises himself thus in the same does better than by hearing the whole Passion or reading all masses. And they are called true Christians who incorporate the life and name of Christ into their own life, as St. Paul says in Gal 5:24: "And they that are of Christ Jesus have crucified the flesh with the passions and the lusts thereof." For Christ's Passion must be dealt with not in words and a show, but in our lives and in truth. Thus St. Paul admonishes us in Heb. 12:3: "For consider him that hath endured such gainsaying of sinners against himself, that ye wax not weary, fainting in your souls;" and St. Peter in his 1st Epistle 4:1: "As Christ suffered in the flesh, arm ye yourselves also with the same mind." But this kind of meditation is now out of use and very rare, although the Epistles of St. Paul and St. Peter are full of it. We have changed the essence into a mere show, and painted the meditation of Christ's sufferings only in letters and on walls.

Enemies of the Cross of Christ & the Christian's Citizenship in Heaven.

PHILIPPIANS 3:17-21: Brethren, join in imitating me, and mark those who so live as you have an example in us. For many, of whom I have often told you and now tell you even with tears, live as enemies of the cross of Christ. Their end is destruction, their god is the belly, and they glory in their shame, with minds set on earthly things. But our commonwealth is in heaven, and from it we await a Savior, the Lord Jesus Christ, who will change our lowly body to be like his glorious body, by the power which enables him even to subject all things to himself.

1. Paul immeasurably extols the Philippians for having made a good beginning in the holy Gospel and for having acquitted themselves commendably, like men in earnest, as manifest by their fruits of faith. The reason he shows this sincere and strong concern for them is his desire that they remain steadfast, not being led astray by false teachers among the roaming Jews. For at that time many Jews went about with the intent of perverting Paul's converts, pretending they taught something far better; while they drew the people away from Christ and back to the Law, for the purpose of establishing and extending their Jewish doctrines.Paul, contemplating with special interest and pleasure his Church of the Philippians, is moved by parental care to admonish them—lest they sometime be misled by such teachers—to hold steadily to what they have received, not seeking anything else and not imagining, like self-secure, besotted souls who allow themselves to be deceived by the devil—not imagining themselves perfect and with complete understanding in all things. In the verses just preceding our text he speaks of himself as having not yet attained to full knowledge.

Purity of Doctrine Enjoined.

2. He particularly admonishes them to follow him and to mark those ministers who walk as he does; also to shape their belief and conduct by the pattern they have received from him. Not only of himself does he make an example, but introduces them who similarly walk, several of whom he mentions in this letter to the Philippians. The individuals whom be bids them

observe and follow must have been persons of special eminence. But it is particularly the doctrine the apostle would have the Philippians pattern after. Therefore we should be chiefly concerned about preserving the purity of the office of the ministry and the genuineness of faith. When these are kept unsullied, doctrine will be right, and good works spontaneous. Later on, in chapter 4, verse 8, Paul admonishes, with reference to the same subject: "If there be any virtue, and if there be any praise, think on these things."

3. Apparently Paul is a rash man to dare boast himself a pattern for all. Other ministers might well accuse him of desiring to exalt his individual self above others. "Think you," our wise ones would say to him, "that you alone have the Holy Spirit, or that no one else is as eager for honor as yourself?" Just so did Miriam and Aaron murmur against Moses, their own brother, saying: "Hath Jehovah indeed spoken only with Moses, hath he not spoken also with us?" (Num. 12:2). And it would seem as if Paul had too high an appreciation of his own character did he hold up his individual self as a pattern, intimating that no one was to be noted as worthy unless he walked as he did; though there might be some who apparently gave greater evidence of the Spirit, of holiness, humility and other graces, than himself, and yet walked not in his way.

4. But he does not say "I, Paul, alone." He says, "as ye have us for an example," that does not exclude other true apostles and teachers. He is admonishing his Church, as he everywhere does, to hold fast to the one true doctrine received from him in the beginning. They are not to be too confident of their own wisdom in the matter, or to presume they have independent authority; but rather to guard against pretenders to a superior doctrine, for so had some been misled.

Righteousness of the Law Is Vain.

5. In what respect he was a pattern or example to them, he has made plain; for instance, in the beginning of this chapter, in the third verse and following, he says: "For we are the circumcision, who worship by the Spirit of God, and glory in Christ Jesus, and have no confidence in the flesh: though I myself might have confidence even in the flesh: if any other man thinketh to have confidence in the flesh, I yet more: circumcised the eighth day, of the stock of Israel, of the tribe of Benjamin, a Hebrew of Hebrews." That is, he commands the highest honor a Jew can boast. "As touching the law," he goes on, "a Pharisee; as touching zeal, persecuting the Church, as touching the righteousness which is in the law, found blameless. Howbeit what things were gain to me, these have I counted loss for Christ. Yea verily, and I count all things to be loss for the excellency of the knowledge of Christ Jesus my Lord: for who I suffered the loss of all things, and do count them but refuse, that I may gain Christ, and be found in him, not having a righteousness of mine own, even that which is of the law, but that which is through faith in Christ, the righteousness which is from God by faith."

6. "Behold, this is the picture or pattern," he would say, "which we hold up for you to follow, that remembering how you obtained righteousness you may hold to it—a righteousness not of the Law." So far as the righteousness of the Law is concerned, Paul dares to say he regards it as filth and refuse (that proceeds from the human body); notwithstanding in its beautiful and blameless form it may be unsurpassed by anything in the world—such righteousness as was manifest in sincere Jews, and in Paul himself before his conversion; for these in their great holiness, regarded Christians as knaves and meriting damnation, and consequently took delight in being party to the persecution and murder of Christians.

7. "Yet," Paul would say, "I who am a Jew by birth have counted all this merit as simply loss that I might be found in 'the righteousness which is from God by faith.'" Only the righteousness of faith teaches us how to apprehend God—how to confidently console ourselves with his grace and await a future life, expecting to approach Christ in the resurrection. By "approaching" him we mean to meet him in death and at the judgment day without terror, not fleeing but gladly drawing near and hailing him with joy as one waited for with intense longing.

Now, the righteousness of the Law cannot effect such confidence of mind. Hence, for me it avails nothing before God; rather it is a detriment. What does avail is God's imputation of righteousness for Christ's sake, through faith. God declares to us in his Word that the believer in his Son shall, for Christ's own sake, have God's grace and eternal life. He who knows this is able to wait in hope for the last day, having no fear, no disposition to flee.

8. But is it not treating the righteousness of the Law with irreverence and contempt to regard it—and so teach as something not only useless and even obstructive, but injurious, loathsome and abominable? Who would have been able to make such a bold statement, and to censure a life so faultless and conforming so closely to the Law as Paul's, without being pronounced by all men a minion of the devil, had not the apostle made that estimation of it himself? And who is to have any more respect for the righteousness of the Law if we are to preach in that strain?

9. Had Paul confined his denunciations to the righteousness of the world or of the heathen—the righteousness dependent upon reason and controlled by secular government, by laws and regulations—his teaching would not have seemed so irreverent. But he distinctly specifies the righteousness of God's Law, or the Ten Commandments, to which we owe an obligation far above what is due temporal powers, for they teach how to live before God—something no heathenish court of justice, no temporal authority, knows anything about. Should we not condemn as a heretic this preacher who goes beyond his prerogative and dares find fault with the Law of God? who also warns us to shun such as observe it, such as trust in its righteousness, and exalts to

sainthood "enemies of the cross of Christ whose God is the belly"—who serve the appetites instead of God?

10. Paul would say of himself: "I, too, was such a one. In my most perfect righteousness of the Law I was an enemy to and persecutor of the congregation, or Church, of Christ. It was the legitimate fruit of my righteousness that I though I must be party to the most horrible persecution of Christ and his Christians. Thus my holiness made me an actual enemy of Christ and a murderer of his followers. The disposition to injure is a natural result of the righteousness of the Law, as all Scripture history from Cain down testifies, and as we see even in the best of the world who have not come to the knowledge of Christ. Princes, civil authorities in proportion to their wisdom, their godliness and honor are the bitter and intolerant enemies of the Gospel.

11. Of the sensual papistical dolts at Rome, cardinals, bishops, priests and the like, it is not necessary to speak here. Their works are manifest. All honorable secular authorities must confess they are simply abandoned knaves, living shameless lives of open scandal, avarice, arrogance, unchastity, vanity, robbery and wickedness of every kind. Not only are they guilty of such living, but shamelessly endeavor to defend their conduct. They must, then, be regarded enemies of Christ and of all honesty and virtue. Hence every respectable man is justly antagonistic toward them. But, as before said, Paul is not here referring to this class, but to eminent, godly individuals, whose lives are beyond reproach. These very ones, when Christians are encountered, are hostile and heinous enough to be able to forget all their own faults in the sight of God, and to magnify to huge beams the motes we Christians have. In fact, they must style the Gospel heresy and satanic doctrine for the purpose of exalting their own holiness and zeal for God.

Righteousness of the Law Opposes the Cross.

12. The thing seems incredible, and I would not have believed it myself, nor have understood Paul's words here, had I not witnessed it with my own eyes and experienced it. Were the apostle to repeat the charge today, who could conceive that our first, noblest, most respectable, godly and holy people, those whom we might expect, above all others, to accept the Word of God—that they, I say, should be enemies to the Christian doctrine? But the examples before us testify very plainly that the "enemies" the apostle refers to must be the individuals styled godly and worthy princes and noblemen, honorable citizens, learned, wise, intelligent individuals. Yet if these could devour at one bite the "Evangelicals," as they are now called, they would do it.

13. If you ask, Whence such a disposition? I answer, it naturally springs from human righteousness. For every individual who professes human righteousness, and knows nothing of Christ, holds that efficacious before God. He relies upon it and gratifies himself with it, presuming thereby to present a flattering appearance in God's sight and to render himself peculiarly acceptable

to him. From being proud and arrogant toward God, he comes to reject them who are not righteous according to the Law; as illustrated in the instance of the Pharisee (Lk. 18:11-12). But greater is his enmity and more bitter his hatred toward the preaching that dares to censure such righteousness and assert its futility to merit God's grace and eternal life.

14. I myself, and others with me, were dominated by such feelings when, under popery, we claimed to be holy and pious; we must confess the fact. If thirty years ago, when I was a devout, holy monk, holding mass every day and having no thought but that I was in the road leading directly to heaven—if then anyone had accused me—had preached to me the things of this text and pronounced our righteousness—which accorded not strictly with the Law of God, but conformed to human doctrine and was manifestly idolatrous—pronounced it without efficacy and said I was an enemy to the cross of Christ, serving my own sensual appetites, I would immediately have at least helped to find stones for putting to death such a Stephen, or to gather wood for the burning of this worst of heretics.

15. So human nature ever does. The world cannot conduct itself in any other way, when the declaration comes from heaven saying: "True you are a holy man, a great and learned jurist, a conscientious regent, a worthy prince, an honorable citizen, and so on, but with all your authority and your upright character you are going to hell; your every act is offensive and condemned in God's sight. If you would be saved you must become an altogether different man; your mind and heart must be changed." Let this be announced and the fire rises, the Rhine is all ablaze; for the self-righteous regard it an intolerable idea that lives so beautiful, lives devoted to praiseworthy callings, should be publicly censured and condemned by the objectionable preaching of a few insignificant individuals regarded as even pernicious, and according to Paul, as filthy refuse, actual obstacles to eternal life.

16. But you may say: "What? Do you forbid good works? Is it not right to lead an honorable, virtuous life? Do you not acknowledge the necessity of political laws, of civil governments? that upon obedience to them depends the maintenance of discipline, peace and honor? Indeed, do you not admit that God himself commands such institutions and wills their observance, punishing where they are disregarded? Much more would he have his own Law and the Ten Commandments honored, not rejected. How dare you then assert that such righteousness is misleading, and obstructive to eternal life? What consistence is there in teaching people to observe the things of the Law, to be righteous in that respect, and at the same time censuring those things as condemned before God? How can the works of the Law be good and precious, and yet repulsive and productive of evil?"

17. I answer, Paul well knows the world takes its stand on this point of righteousness by the Law, and hence would contradict him. But let him who will, consult the apostle as to why he makes such bold assertions here. For

indeed the words of the text are not our words, but his. True, law and government are essential in temporal life, as Paul himself confesses, and God would have everyone honor and obey them. Indeed, he has ordained their observance among Turks and heathen. Yet it is a fact that these people, even the best and most upright of them, they who lead honorable lives, are naturally in their hearts enemies to Christ, and devote their intellectual powers to exterminating God's people.

It must be universally admitted that the Turks, with all the restrictions and austerity of life imposed upon them by the Koran, a life more rigorous even than that of Christians—it must be admitted they belong to the devil. In other words, we adjudge them condemned with all their righteousness, but at the same time say they do right in punishing thieves, robbers, murderers, drunkards and other offenders; more, that Christians living within their jurisdiction are under obligation to pay tribute, and to serve them with person and property. Precisely the same thing is true respecting our princes who persecute the Gospel and are open enemies to Christ: we must be obedient to them, paying the tribute and rendering the service imposed; yet they, and all obedient followers willingly consenting to the persecution of the Gospel, must be looked upon as condemned before God.

18. Similarly does Paul speak concerning the righteousness of all the Jews and pious saints who are not Christians.His utterance is bold and of certain sound. He censures them and, weeping, deprecatingly refers to certain who direct the people to the righteousness of the law with the sole result of making "enemies to the cross of Christ."

19. Again, all the praise he has for them is to say that their "end is perdition"; they are condemned in spite of strenuous efforts all their lives to teach and enforce the righteousness of works. Here on earth it is truly a priceless distinction, an admirable and noble treasure, a praiseworthy honor, to have the name of being a godly and upright prince, ruler or citizen; a pious, virtuous wife or virgin. Who would not praise and exalt such virtue? It is indeed a rare and valuable thing in the world. But however beautiful, priceless and admirable an honor it is, Paul tells us, it is ultimately condemned and pertains not to heaven.

Human Righteousness Idolatrous.

20. The apostle makes his accusation yet more galling with the words "whose god is their belly." Thus you hear how human righteousness, even at its best, extends no higher than to service of the sensual appetites. Take all the wisdom, justice, jurisprudence, artifice, even the highest virtues the world affords, and what are they? They minister only to that god, carnal appetite. They can go no farther than the needs of this life, their whole purpose being to satisfy physical cravings. When the physical appetites of the worldly pass, they pass likewise, and the gifts and virtues we have mentioned can no longer serve

them. All perish and go to destruction together—righteousness, virtues, laws and physical appetites which they have served as their god. For they are wholly ignorant of the true and eternal God; they know not how to serve him and receive eternal life. So then in its essential features such a life is merely idolatrous, having no greater object than the preservation of this perishable body and its enjoyment of peace and honor.

21. The fourth accusation is, "whose glory is in their shame." That is all their glory amounts to. Let wise philosophers, scrupulous heathen, keen jurists, receive the acme of praise and honor—it is yet but shame. True, their motto is "Love of Virtue"; they boast strong love of virtue and righteousness and may even think themselves sincere. But judged by final results, their boast is without foundation and ends in shame. For the utmost their righteousness can effect is the applause of the world—here on earth. Before God it avails nothing. It cannot touch the life to come. Ultimately it leaves its possessor a captive in shame. Death devours and hell clutches him.

22. You may again object, "If what you say it true, why observe temporal restrictions? Let us live in indulgent carelessness following our inclinations. Let pass the godly, honorable man; the virtuous, upright wife or virgin." I answer, By no means; that is not the design. You have heard it is God's command and will that there be temporal righteousness even among Turks and heathen. And later on (ch. 4, 8) Paul admonishes Christians to "think on these things," that is, on what is true. He says: "Whatsoever things are honorable, whatsoever things are just, whatsoever things are pure, whatsoever things are lovely, whatsoever things are of good report; if there be any virtue, and if there be any praise, think on these things." And continuing, in verse 9, he refers them to his own example, saying, "which ye both learned and received and heard and saw in me."

Fruits of Faith.

23. With the believers in Christ, them who have their righteousness in him, there should follow in this life on earth the fruits of upright living, in obedience to God. These fruits constitute the good works acceptable to God, which, being works of faith and wrought in Christ, will be rewarded in the life to come. But Paul has in mind the individuals who, rejecting faith in Christ, regard their self-directed lives, their humanly-wrought works, which conform to the Law, as righteousness availing in the sight of God. His reference is to them who so trust, though wholly ignorant of Christ, for whose sake, without any merit on our part, righteousness is imputed to us by God. The only condition is we must believe in Christ; for he became man, died for our sins and rose from the dead, for the very purpose of liberating us from our sins and granting us his resurrection and life. Toward the heavenly life we should tend, in our life here walking in harmony with it; as Paul says in conclusion: "Our citizenship is in heaven [not earthly and not confined to this temporal life only]; whence also we

wait for a Saviour, the Lord Jesus Christ."

If we have no knowledge, no consciousness, of this fact, it matters not how beautiful and praiseworthy our human, earthly righteousness may be, it is merely a hindrance and an injury. For flesh and blood cannot help relying on its own righteousness and arrogantly boasting in this strain: "We are better, more honorable, more godly, than others. We Jews are the people of God and keep his Law." Even Christians are not wholly free from the pernicious influence of human holiness. They ever seek to bring their own works and merits before God. I know for myself what pains are inflicted by this godless wisdom, this figment of righteousness, and what effort must be made before the serpent's head is bruised.

24. Now, this is the situation and there is no alternative: Either suffer hell or regard your human righteousness as loss and filth and endeavor not to be found relying on it at your last hour, in the presence of God and judgment, but rather stand in the righteousness of Christ. In the garment of Christ's righteousness and reared in him you may, in the resurrection from sin and death, meet Christ and exclaim: "Hail, beloved Lord and Saviour, thou who hast redeemed me from the wretched body of sin and death, and fashioned me like unto thy holy, pure and glorious body!"

God's Patience with Human Righteousness.

25. Meantime, while we walk in the faith of his righteousness, he has patience with the poor, frail righteousness of this earthly life, which otherwise is but filth in his sight. He honors our human holiness by supporting and protecting it during the time we live on earth; just as we honor our corrupt, filthy bodies, adorning them with beautiful,costly garments and golden ornaments, and reposing them on cushions and beds of luxury. Though but stench and filth encased in flesh, they are honored above everything else on earth. For their sake are all things performed—the ordering and ruling, building and laboring; and God himself permits sun and moon to shine that they may receive light and heat, and everything to grow on earth for their benefit. What is the human body but a beautiful pyx containing that filthy, repulsive object of reverence, the digestive organs, which the body must always patiently carry about; yes, which we must even nourish and minister to, glad if only they perform their functions properly?

26. Similarly God deals with us. Because he would confer eternal life upon man, he patiently endures the filthy righteousness of this life wherein we must dwell until the last day, for the sake of his chosen people and until the number is complete. For so long as the final day is deferred, not all to have eternal life are yet born. When the time shall be fulfilled, the number completed, God will suddenly bring to an end the world with its governments, its jurists and authorities, its conditions of life; in short, he will utterly abolish earthly righteousness, destroying physical appetites and all else together. For every

form of human holiness is condemned to destruction; yet for the sake of Christians, to whom eternal life is appointed, and for their sake only, all these must be perpetuated until the last saint is born and has attained life everlasting. Were there but one saint yet to be born, for the sake of that one the world must remain. For God regards not the world nor has he need for it, except for the sake of his Christians.

27. Therefore, when God enjoins upon us obedience to the emperor, and godly, honest lives on earth, it is no warrant that our subjection to temporal authority is to continue forever. Instead, God necessarily will minister to, adorn and honor this wretched body—vile body, as Paul here has it—with power and dominion. Yet the apostle terms human righteousness "filth," and says it is not necessary to God's kingdom; indeed, that it is condemned in the sight of God with all its honor and glory, and all the world must be ashamed of it in his presence, confessing themselves guilty. Paul in Romans 3:27 and 4:2 testifies to this fact when he tells how even the exalted, holy fathers—Abraham, and others—though having glory before the world because of their righteous works, could not make them serve to obtain honor before God. Much less will worldly honor avail with God in the case of individuals who, being called honorable, pious, honest, virtuous—lords and princes, wives and husbands—boast of such righteousness.

28. Outwardly, then, though your righteousness may appear dazzlingly beautiful before the world, inwardly you are but filth. Illustrative of this point is the story told of a certain nun regarded holy above all others. She would not fellowship with anyone else, but sat alone in her cell in wrapt devotion, praying unceasingly. She boasted special revelations and visions and had no consciousness of anything but that beloved angels hovered about and adorned her with a golden crown. But some outside, ardently desiring to behold such sights, peeped through holes and crevices, and seeing her head but defiled with filth, laughed at her.

29. Notice, the reason Paul calls the righteousness of the Law filth and pollution, is his desire to denounce the honor and glory claimed for it in God's sight; notwithstanding he honors before the world the observance of the Law by styling it "righteousness." But if you ostentatiously boast of such righteousness to him, he pronounces his sentence of judgment making you an abomination, an enemy of the cross of Christ, and shaming your boasted honor and finally casting you into hell. Concerning the righteousness of faith, however, which in Christ avails before God, he says: "Our citizenship [conversation] is in heaven, from whence also we look for the Saviour, the Lord Jesus Christ; who shall change our vile body, that it may be fashioned like unto his glorious body."

30. We who are baptized and believe in Christ, Paul's thought is, do not base our works and our hope on the righteouness of this temporal life. Through faith in Christ, we have a righteousness that holds in heaven. It abides in Christ

alone; otherwise it would avail naught before God. And our whole concern is to be eternally in Christ; to have our earthly existence culminate in yonder life when Christ shall come and change this life into another, altogether new, pure, holy and like unto his own, with a life and a body having the nature of his.

The Christian a Citizen of Heaven.

31. Therefore we are no longer citizens of earth. The baptized Christian is born a citizen of heaven through baptism. We should be mindful of this fact and walk here as if native there. We are to console ourselves with the fact that God thus accepts us and will transplant us there. Meantime we must await the coming again of the Saviour, who is to bring from heaven to us eternal righteousness, life, honor and glory.

32. We are baptized and made Christians, not to the end that we may have great honor, or renown of righteousness, or earthly dominion, power and possessions. Notwithstanding we do have these because they are requisite to our physical life, yet we are to regard them as mere filth, wherewith we minister to our bodily welfare as best we can for the benefit of posterity. We Christians, however, are expectantly to await the coming of the Saviour. His coming will not be to our injury or shame as it may be in the case of others. He comes for the salvation of our unprofitable, impotent bodies. Wretchedly worthless as they are in this life, they are much more unprofitable when lifeless and perishing in the earth.

33. But, however miserable, powerless and contemptible in life and death, Christ will at his coming render our bodies beautiful, pure, shining and worthy of honor, until they correspond to his own immortal, glorious body. Not like it as it hung on the cross or lay in the grave, bloodstained, livid and disgraced; but as it is now, glorified at the Father's right hand. We need not, then, be alarmed at the necessity of laying aside our earthly bodies; at being despoiled of the honor, righteousness and life adhering in them, to deliver it to the devouring power of death and the grave—something well calculated to terrify the enemies of Christ: but we may joyfully hope for and await his speedy coming to deliver us from this miserable, filthy pollution.

"According to the working whereby he is able even to subdue all things unto himself."

The Glorified Body of the Christian.

34. Think of the honor and the glory Christ's righteousness brings even to our bodies! How can this poor, sinful, miserable, filthy, polluted body become like unto that of the Son of God, the Lord of Glory? What are you—your powers and abilities, or those of all men, to effect this glorious thing? But Paul says human righteousness, merit, glory and power have nothing to do with it. They are mere filth and pollution, and condemned as well. Another force intervenes,

the power of Christ the Lord, who is able to bring all things into subjection to himself. Now, if he has power to subject all things unto himself at will, he is also able to glorify the pollution and filth of this wretched body, even when it has become worms and dust. In his hands it is as clay in the hands of the potter, and from the polluted lump of clay he can make a vessel that shall be a beautiful, new, pure, glorious body, surpassing the sun in its brilliance and beauty.

35. Through baptism Christ has taken us into his hands, actually that he may exchange our sinful, condemned, perishable, physical lives for the new, imperishable righteousness and life he prepares for body and soul. Such is the power and the agency exalting us to marvelous glory—something no earthly righteousness of the Law could accomplish. The righteousness of the Law leaves our bodies to shame and destruction; it reaches not beyond physical existence. But the righteousness of Christ inspires with power, making evident that we worship not the body but the true and living God, who does not leave us to shame and destruction, but delivers from sin, death and condemnation, and exalts this perishable body to eternal honor and glory.

Christ Our Great High Priest

HEBREWS 9:11-15: But Christ being come an high priest of good things to come, by a greater and more perfect tabernacle, not made with hands, that is to say, not of this building; Neither by the blood of goats and calves, but by his own blood he entered in once into the holy place, having obtained eternal redemption for us. For if the blood of bulls and of goats, and the ashes of an heifer sprinkling the unclean, sanctifieth to the purifying of the flesh: How much more shall the blood of Christ, who through the eternal Spirit offered himself without spot to God, purge your conscience from dead works to serve the living God? And for this cause he is the mediator of the new testament, that by means of death, for the redemption of the transgressions that were under the first testament, they which are called might receive the promise of eternal inheritance.

1. An understanding of practically all of the Epistle to the Hebrews is necessary before we can hope to make this text clear to ourselves. Briefly, the epistle treats of a twofold priesthood. The former priesthood was a material one, with material adornment, tabernacle, sacrifices and with pardon couched in ritual; material were all its appointments. The new order is a spiritual priesthood, with spiritual adornments, spiritual tabernacle and sacrifices—spiritual in all that pertains to it. Christ, in the exercise of his priestly office, in the sacrifice on the cross, was not adorned with silk and gold and precious stones, but with divine love, wisdom, patience, obedience and all virtues. His adornment was apparent to none but God and possessors, of the Spirit, for it was spiritual.

2. Christ sacrificed not goats nor calves nor birds; not bread; not blood nor flesh, as did Aaron and his posterity: he offered his own body and blood, and the manner of the sacrifice was spiritual; for it took place through the Holy Spirit, as here stated. Though the body and blood of Christ were visible the same as any other material object, the fact that he offered them as a sacrifice was not apparent. It was not a visible sacrifice, as in the case of offerings at the hands of Aaron. Then the goat or calf, the flesh and blood, were material sacrifices visibly offered, and recognized as sacrifices. But Christ offered himself in the heart before God. His sacrifice was perceptible to no mortal. Therefore, his bodily flesh and blood becomes a spiritual sacrifice. Similarly, we Christians,

the posterity of Christ our Aaron, offer up our own bodies (Rom 12:1). And our offering is likewise a spiritual sacrifice, or, as Paul has it, a "reasonable service"; for we make it in spirit, and it is beheld of God alone.

3. Again, in the new order, the tabernacle or house is spiritual; for it is heaven, or the presence of God. Christ hung upon a cross; he was not offered in a temple. He was offered before the eyes of God, and there he still abides. The cross is an altar in a spiritual sense. The material cross was indeed visible, but none knew it as Christ's altar. Again, his prayer, his sprinkled blood, his burnt incense, were all spiritual, for it was all wrought through his spirit.

4. Accordingly, the fruit and blessing of his office and sacrifice, the forgiveness of our sins and our justification, are likewise spiritual. In the Old Covenant, the priest with his sacrifices and sprinklings of blood effected merely as it were an external absolution, or pardon, corresponding to the childhood stage of the people. The recipient was permitted to move publicly among the people; he was externally holy and as one restored from excommunication. He who failed to obtain absolution from the priest was unholy, being denied membership in the congregation and enjoyment of its privileges; in all respects he was separated like those in the ban today.

5. But such absolution rendered no one inwardly holy and just before God. Something beyond that was necessary to secure true forgiveness. It was the same principle which governs church discipline today. He who has received no more than the remission, or absolution, of the ecclesiastical judge will surely remain forever out of heaven. On the other hand, he who is in the ban of the Church is hellward bound only when the sentence is confirmed at a higher tribunal. I can make no better comparison than to say that it was the same in the old Jewish priesthood as now in the Papal priesthood, which, with its loosing and binding, can prohibit or permit only external communion among Christians. It is true, God required such measures in the time of the Jewish dispensation, that he might restrain by fear; just as now he sanctions church discipline when rightly employed, in order to punish and restrain the evil-doer, though it has no power in itself to raise people to holiness or to push them into wickedness.

6. But with the priesthood of Christ is true spiritual remission, sanctification and absolution. These avail before God—God grant that it be true of us—whether we be outwardly excommunicated, or holy, or not. Christ's blood has obtained for us pardon forever acceptable with God. God will forgive our sins for the sake of that blood so long as its power shall last and its intercession for grace in our behalf, which is forever. Therefore, we are forever holy and blessed before God. This is the substance of the text. Now that we shall find it easy to understand, we will briefly consider it.

"But Christ having come a high priest of the good things to come."

7. The adornment of Aaron and his descendants, the high priests, was of a material nature, and they obtained for the people a merely formal remission of

sins, performing their office in a perishable temple, or tabernacle. It was evident to men that their absolution and sanctification before the congregation was a temporal blessing confined to the present. But when Christ came upon the cross no one beheld him as he went before God in the Holy Spirit, adorned with every grace and virtue, a true High Priest. The blessings wrought by him are not temporal—a merely formal pardon—but the "blessings to come"; namely, blessings which are spiritual and eternal. Paul speaks of them as blessings to come, not that we are to await the life to come before we can have forgiveness and all the blessings of divine grace, but because now we possess them only in faith. They are as yet hidden, to be revealed in the future life. Again, the blessings we have in Christ were, from the standpoint of the Old Testament priesthood, blessings to come.

"Through the greater and more perfect tabernacle, not made with hands, that is to say, not of this creation.

8. The apostle does not name the tabernacle he mentions; nor can he, so strange its nature! It exists only in the sight of God, and is ours in faith, to be revealed hereafter. It is not made with hands, like the Jewish tabernacle; in other words, not of "this building." The old tabernacle, like all buildings of its nature, necessarily was made of wood and other temporal materials created by God. God says in Isaiah 66:1-2: "What manner of house will ye build unto me?....For all these things hath my hand made, and so all these things came to be." But that greater tabernacle has not yet form; it is not yet finished. God is building it and he shall reveal it. Christ's words are (Jn. 14:3), "And if I go and prepare a place for you."

"Nor yet through the blood of goats and calves, but through his own blood, entered in once for all into the holy place, having obtained eternal redemption."

9. According to Leviticus 16, the high priest must once a year enter into the holy place with the blood of rams and other offerings, and with these make formal reconciliation for the people. This ceremony typified that Christ, the true Priest, should once die for us, to obtain for us the true atonement. But the former sacrifice, having to be repeated every year, was but a temporary and imperfect atonement; it did not eternally suffice, as does the atonement of Christ. For though we fall and sin repeatedly, we have confidence that the blood of Christ does not fall, or sin; it remains steadfast before God, and the expiation is perpetual and eternal. Under its sway grace is perpetually renewed, without work or merit on our part, provided we do not stand aloof in unbelief.

"For if the blood of goats and bulls, and the ashes of a heifer," etc.

10. Concerning the water of separation and the ashes of the red heifer, read Numbers 19; and concerning the blood of bulls and goats, Leviticus 16:14-15. According to Paul, these were formal and temporal purifications, as I stated above. But Christ, in God's sight, purifies the conscience of dead works; that is, of sins meriting death, and of works performed in sin and therefore dead. Christ purifies from these, that we may serve the living God by living works.

"And for this cause he is the mediator of a new covenant [testament]," etc.

11. Under the old law, which provided only for formal, or ritualistic pardon, and restored to human fellowship, sin and transgressions remained, burdening the conscience. It—the old law—did not benefit the soul at all, inasmuch as God did not institute it to purify and safeguard the conscience, nor to bestow the Spirit. It existed merely for the purpose of outward discipline, restraint and correction. So Paul teaches that under the Old Testament dispensation man's transgressions remained, but now Christ is our Mediator through his blood; by it our conscience, is freed from sin in the sight of God, inasmuch as God promises the Spirit through the blood of Christ. All, however, do not receive him. Only those called to be heirs eternal, the elect, receive the Spirit.

12. We find, then, in this excellent lesson, the comforting doctrine taught that Christ is he whom we should know as the Priest and Bishop of our souls; that no sin is forgiven, nor the Holy Spirit given, by reason of works or merit on our part, but alone through the blood of Christ, and that to those for whom God has ordained it. This matter has been sufficiently set forth in the various postils.

On Faith & Coming to Christ

On Faith and Coming to Christ, and the True Bread of Heaven:

JOHN 6:44-55: No man can come to me, except the Father which hath sent me draw him: and I will raise him up at the last day. It is written in the prophets, And they shall be all taught of God. Every man therefore that hath heard, and hath learned of the Father, cometh unto me. Not that any man hath seen the Father, save he which is of God, he hath seen the Father. Verily, verily, I say unto you, He that believeth on me hath everlasting life. I am that bread of life. Your fathers did eat manna in the wilderness, and are dead. This is the bread which cometh down from heaven, that a man may eat thereof, and not die. I am the living bread which came down from heaven: if any man eat of this bread, he shall live for ever: and the bread that I will give is my flesh, which I will give for the life of the world. The Jews therefore strove among themselves, saying, How can this man give us his flesh to eat? Then Jesus said unto them, Verily, verily, I say unto you, Except ye eat the flesh of the Son of man, and drink his blood, ye have no life in you. Whoso eateth my flesh, and drinketh my blood, hath eternal life; and I will raise him up at the last day. For my flesh is meat indeed, and my blood is drink indeed.

Section I. On Faith, and Coming to Christ.

1. This Gospel text teaches exclusively of the Christian faith, and awakens that faith in us; just as John, throughout his whole Gospel, simply instructs us how to trust in Christ the Lord. This faith alone, when based upon the sure promises of God, must save us; as our text clearly explains. And in the light of it all, they must become fools who have taught us other ways to become godly.

All that human ingenuity can devise, be it as holy and as luminous as it may, must tumble to the ground if man be saved in God's way—in a way different from that which man himself plans. Man may forever do as he will, he can never enter heaven unless God takes the first step with his Word, which offers him divine grace and enlightens his heart so as to get upon the right way.

2. This right way, however, is the Lord Jesus Christ. Whoever desires to seek another way, as the great multitudes venture to do by means of their own works, has already missed the right way; for Paul says to the Galatians: "If righteousness is through the Law," that is, through the works of the Law, "then Christ died for naught" (Gal. 2:21). Therefore I say man must fall upon this Gospel and be broken to pieces and in deep consciousness lie prostrate, like a man that is powerless, unable to move hand or foot. He must only lie motionless and cry: Almighty God, merciful Father, now help me! I cannot help myself. Christ, my Lord, do help now, for with only my own effort all is lost! Thus, in the light of this cornerstone, which is Christ, everyone becomes as nothing; as Christ says of himself in Luke 20:17-18, when he asks the Pharisees and scribes: "What then is this that is written. The stone which the builders rejected, the same was made the head of the corner? Every one that falleth on that stone shall be 'broken to pieces; but on whomsoever it shall fall, it will scatter him as dust" (Ps. 118:22). Therefore, we must either fall upon this stone, Christ, in all our inability and helplessness, rejecting our own merits, and be broken to pieces, or he will forever crush us by his severe sentence and judgment. It is better that we fall upon him than that he should fall upon us. For this reason the Lord says in this Gospel: "No man can come to me, except the Father that sent me draw him: and I will raise him up in the last day."

3. He must surely perish whom the rather does not draw. Thus it is decreed, that whoever does not come to this Son must be condemned forever. The Son is given to us only to the end that he may save us; besides him, nothing saves us, either in heaven or on earth. If he does not help us, then nothing will. On this Peter says in the Acts of the Apostles (4:11-12): "He is the stone which was set at naught of you the builders, which was made the head of the corner. And in none other is there salvation; neither is there any other name underheaven, that is given among men, wherein we must be saved." Where, in the light of this, are our theologians and professors who taught us that we become pious through our many good works? Here the great master Aristotle is put to shame, who proclaimed that reason strives for the best and always follows after the good. Christ says to this: No; if the rather comes not first and draws men, they must forever perish.

4. Here all men must confess their incapacity and inability to do the good. Should one imagine he is able to do anything good of his own strength he does no less than make Christ the Lord a liar; he would rudely and defiantly come to the Father and in all rashness ascend to heaven. Therefore, where the pure and plain Word of God goes, it breaks into pieces everything that is exalted of

man, it makes valleys of all their mountains, and all their hills it makes low, as the prophet Isaiah (40:4) says. Every heart that hears this Word must lose faith in itself, else it will not be able to come to Christ. God's works do nothing but destroy and make alive, condemn and minister salvation. Hannah, the mother of Samuel, sings of the Lord: "Jehovah killeth, and maketh alive; he bringeth down to the grave and bringeth up" (1 Sam. 2:6).

5. Hence, a person who is thus smitten in his heart, by God, to confess that he is one who, on account of his sins, must be condemned, is like the righteous man whom with the first words of this Gospel God wounds, and because of that wound fixes upon him the band or cord of his divine grace, by which he draws him, so that he must seek help and counsel for his soul. Before he could not obtain any help or counsel from God, nor did he ever desire it; but now he finds the first comfort and promise of God, which Luke 2:10 records thus: "For every one that asketh receiveth; and he that seeketh findeth; and to him that knocketh it shall be opened." From such promises will he ever continue to gain courage as long as he lives, and will ever win greater and greater confidence in God. Just as soon as he hears that grace is the work of God alone, he will desire it of God as from the hand of his gracious Father, who wishes to draw him. Now, if he is drawn by God to Christ, he will certainly experience what the Lord here says: "He will raise him up in the last day." For he has laid hold upon the Word of God and trusts God. In this he has a sure sign that he is one whom God has drawn, as John says in his First Epistle (5:10): "He that believeth on the Son of God hath the witness in him."

6. Hence, it must necessarily follow that he is taught of God, and that he knows now in truth that the meaning of God is nothing more than Helper, Comforter, Saviour, as we say of those who rescue us from danger: Thou wast today my God. From this it is now clear that God will be to us nothing less than a saviour, a helper, and a giver of all blessedness, who neither demands nor desires anything from us. He only gives, he only offers to us; as he says to Israel in Ps. 81:10: "I am Jehovah thy God, who brought thee up out of the land of Egypt: open thy mouth wide, and I will fill it." Who would not be kindly disposed to such a God, who approaches us so lovingly and graciously, and offers us his favor and blessings if we only acknowledge him as God and are willing to be taught of him? They cannot escape the severe, eternal judgment of God who ignore such grace, as the Epistle to the Hebrews (10:28-29) says: "A man that hath set at naught Moses' law dieth without compassion: of how much sorer punishment, think ye, shall he be judged worthy, who hath trodden under foot the Son of God, and hath counted the blood of the covenant wherewith he was sanctified an unholy thing."

7. Oh, how diligent and earnest St. Paul is in all his Epistles that we may always grasp the knowledge of God aright! How often he expresses the wish for growth in the knowledge of God! As if he would say: If you only knew and understood what God is, then you would be already saved, then you would gain

love for him and do only those things well pleasing to him. Thus he says to the Colossians (1:9-12): "For this cause we also, since the day we heard it, do not cease to pray and make request for you, that ye may be filled with the knowledge of his will in all spiritual wisdom and understanding, to walk worthily of the Lord unto all pleasing, bearing fruit in every good work, and increasing in knowledge of God; strengthened with all power, according to the might of his glory, unto all patience and longsuffering with joy; giving thanks unto the Father, who made us meet to be partakers of the inheritance of the saints in light." And in Ps. 119:34 David says: "Give me understanding, and I shall keep thy Law; yea, I shall observe it with my whole heart."

8. Thus you learn from the first utterance in today's Gospel that this knowledge must come from God the Father; he must lay the first stone of the foundation in us, else we will never do anything. But this is accomplished in the following way: God sends us preachers, whom he has taught, to preach to us his will. First he instructs us that our entire lives and characters, however beautiful and holy they may be, are before him as nothing, yea, are as abomination, and displeasing; this is called a preaching of the Law. Then he offers us grace; that is, he tells us that he will not utterly condemn and reject us, but will receive us in his beloved Son, and not merely receive us, but make us heirs of his kingdom, lords over all that is in heaven and upon earth. This is called preaching grace or preaching the Gospel. But God is the origin of all; he first awakens preachers and constrains them to preach. This is the meaning of St. Paul's words when he says to the Romans: "So belief cometh of hearing, and hearing by the Word of Christ" (Rom. 10:17). This truth the words of the Lord in today's Gospel also declares, when Christ says: "It is written in the prophets, And they shall all be taught of God. Every one that hath heard from the Father, and hath learned, cometh unto me. Not that any man hath seen the Father, save he that is from God, he hath seen the Father."

9. Now, under the first preaching, the preaching of the Law, namely, that we with all our works are condemned, man is restless and fearful before God, and knows not what to do with his life and deeds. He suffers from an accusing and timid conscience, and if relief from some source were not to come quickly he would have to despair forever. Therefore, we must not long delay with the other preaching; we must preach the Gospel to him and lead him to Christ as the one whom the Father has given to us to be our mediator, that we should be saved solely through him, out of pure grace and mercy, without any works or merit on our part. The heart rejoices at this word and runs to such grace as a thirsty deer to the water. This longing David keenly experiences when he says in Ps. 42:1-2: "As the heart panteth after the water brooks, so panteth my soul after thee, O God, my soul thirsteth for God, for the living God."

10. Now, when one comes to Christ, that is, to his Gospel, he hears the personal voice of Christ the Lord, which confirms the knowledge God taught him, namely, that God is nothing but a very gracious Saviour, who wants to be

gracious and merciful to all who call upon him. Therefore, the Lord adds:

"Verily verily, I say unto you, He that believeth hath eternal life. I am the bread of life. Your fathers ate the manna in the wilderness, and they died. This is the bread that cometh down out of heaven, that a man may eat thereof, and not die. I am the living bread that came down out of heaven: if any man eat of this bread, he shall live forever: yea and the bread which I will give is my flesh, for the life of the world."

11. In these words the soul finds a well prepared table, at which it satisfies all hunger; for it knows for a certainty that he who speaks these words cannot lie. Therefore the soul falls upon the Word, clings to it, trusts in it, and also builds its dwelling-place in the strength of this well-prepared table. This is the feast for which the heavenly Father slayed his oxen and fatlings and invited us all to it.

SECTION II. The Bread Of Heaven.

12. The living bread, of which the Lord here speaks, is Christ himself, of whom we partake. If in our hearts we lay hold of only a morsel of this bread, we shall have forever enough and can never be separated from God. The partaking of this bread is nothing but faith in Christ our Lord, that he is, as Paul says in 1 Cor. 1:30, "made unto us wisdom from God, and righteousness and sanctification, and redemption." He who eats of this food lives forever. Therefore, the Lord says, immediately following this Gospel lesson, where the Jews strove among themselves about this discourse of his: "Verily, verily, I say unto you, Except ye eat the flesh of the Son of man and drink his blood, ye have not life in yourselves. He that eateth my flesh and drinketh my blood hath eternal life; and I will raise him up at the last day."

13. The bread from heaven the fathers ate in the wilderness, as Christ says here, was powerless to keep them from dying; but this bread makes immortal. If we believe on Christ, death cannot harm us; yea, it is no longer death. The Lord utters the same truth in another passage when he says to the Jews: "Verily, verily, I say unto you, If a man keep my Word, he shall never see death" (John 8:51). Here he speaks definitely of the Word of faith, and of the Gospel.

14. But one may say, as did the Jews, who took offense at these words of the Lord: The saints, nevertheless, died, and Abraham and the prophets likewise died. We reply to this: The death of Christians is only a sleep, as the Scriptures everywhere call it. A Christian neither tastes nor sees death; that is, he is never conscious of any death; for this Saviour, Christ Jesus, in whom he believes, has destroyed death so that he no longer needs to taste it and pay its penalty. Death is to the Christians only a transition of life, yea, a door to life: as Christ says in John 5:24: "Verily, verily, I say unto you, He that heareth my Word, and believeth him that sent me, hath eternal life., and cometh not into judgment, but hath passed out of death into life."

15. Therefore, a Christian life is a life of bliss and joy. Christ's yoke is easy

and sweet; the reason it seems to us galling and heavy is that the Father has not yet drawn us. and so we have no pleasure in it, neither does this Gospel lesson minister comfort to us. If we, however, rightly appropriated the words of Christ, they would be of much greater comfort to us. By faith we partake of this bread that has come down from heaven, Christ the Lord, when we believe on him as our Saviour and Redeemer.

16. In this light I now remind you that these words are not to be misconstrued and made to refer to the Sacrament of the Altar; whoever so interprets them does violence to this Gospel text. There is not a letter in it that refers to the Lord's Supper. Why should Christ here have in mind that Sacrament when it was not yet instituted? The whole chapter from which this Gospel is taken speaks of nothing but the spiritual food, namely, faith. When the people followed the Lord merely hoping again to eat and drink, as the Lord himself charges them with doing, he took the figure from the temporal food they sought, and speaks throughout the entire chapter of a spiritual food. He says: "The words that I have spoken unto you are spirit, and are life." Thereby he shows that he feeds them with the object of inducing them to believe on him, and that as they partook of the temporal food, so should they also partake of the spiritual. On this subject we will say more at some other time.

17. Now let us here notice that the Lord approaches us so lovingly and graciously, and offers us himself—his flesh and blood—in such gentle words that it should in all reason move the heart to believe on him; to believe that this bread, his flesh and blood, born of the Virgin Mary, was given because he had to pay the penalty of death and suffer in our stead the torments of hell, and, besides, to suffer the guilt of sins he never committed, as if they were his own. This he did willingly and received us as brethren and sisters. If we believe this we do the will of the heavenly Father, which is nothing else than that we believe on the Son. Christ says, just before our text: "This is the will of my Father, that every one that beholdeth the Son, and believeth on him, should have eternal life; and I will raise him up at the last day" (I John 6:40).

18. It is now evident that whoever has faith in this bread of heaven—in Christ, in this flesh and blood, of which he here speaks that it is given to him and that it is his—he also accepts it as his own, and has already done the will of God and eaten of this heavenly manna; as Augustine says: What do you prepare for your mouth? Only believe, and you have already eaten.

19. The whole New Testament treats of this spiritual supper, and especially does John here. The Sacrament of the Altar is a testament and confirmation of this true supper, with which we should strengthen our faith and be assured that this body and this blood, which we receive in the Sacrament has rescued us from sin and death, the devil, hell and all misery. Concerning this I have spoken and written more on other occasions.

20. What is the proof by which one may know that this heavenly bread is his and that he is invited to such a spiritual supper? He needs only to look at his

own heart. If he finds it so disposed that it is softened and cheered by God's promises and is firm in the conviction that it may appropriate this
bread of life, then he may be assured that he is one of the invited; for as one believes, even so is it done unto him. >From that moment on, he loves his neighbor and helps him as his brother; he rescues him, gives to him, loans to him and does nothing for him but that which he would desire his neighbor to do for himself. All this is attributable to the fact that Christ's kindness to him has leavened his heart with sweetness and love, so that he has pleasure and joy in serving his neighbor; yea, he is even in misery if he has no one to whom to show kindness. Besides all this, he is gently and humbly disposed toward everybody; he does not highly esteem the transient pomps of the world; he accepts everyone as he is, speaks evil of no one, interprets all things for the best where he sees things are not going right. When his neighbors are lacking in faith, in love, in life, then he prays for them, and he is heartily sorry when anyone gives offense to God or to his neighbor. To sum up all, with him the root and sap are good, for he is grafted into a rich and fruitful vine, in Christ; therefore, such fruits must come forth.

21. But if one has not faith and is not taught of God—if he never eats of this bread from heaven—he surely never brings forth these fruits. For where such fruits are not produced, there is certainly no true faith. St. Peter teaches us in 2 Peter 1:10 that we should make our calling unto salvation sure by good works; there he is really speaking of the works of love, of serving one's neighbor and treating him as one's own flesh and blood. This is sufficient on this Gospel. Let us pray for God's grace.

Of The Office of Preaching

Of the Office of Preaching & of Preachers and Hearers:

JOHN 10: 1-11: Verily, verily, I say unto you, He that entereth not by the door into the sheepfold, but climbeth up some other way, the same is a thief and a robber. But he that entereth in by the door is the shepherd of the sheep. To him the porter openeth; and the sheep hear his voice: and he calleth his own sheep by name, and leadeth them out. And when he putteth forth his own sheep, he goeth before them, and the sheep follow him: for they know his voice. And a stranger will they not follow, but will flee from him: for they know not the voice of strangers. This parable spake Jesus unto them: but they understood not what things they were which he spake unto them. Then said Jesus unto them again, Verily, verily, I say unto you, I am the door of the sheep. All that ever came before me are thieves and robbers: but the sheep did not hear them. I am the door: by me if any man enter in, he shall be saved, and shall go in and out, and find pasture. The thief cometh not, but for to steal, and to kill, and to destroy: I am come that they might have life, and that they might have it more abundantly. I am the good shepherd: the good shepherd giveth his life for the sheep.

Section I. True Preachers of the Word must Be Regularly Called.

1. This Gospel treats of the office of the ministry, how it is constituted, what it accomplishes and how it is misused. It is indeed very necessary to know these things, for the office of preaching is second to none in Christendom. St. Paul highly esteemed this office for the reason that through it the Word of God was proclaimed which is effective to the salvation of all who believe it. He says to the Romans (1:16): "I am not ashamed of the Gospel, for it is the power of God unto salvation to every one that believeth." We must now consider this theme, since our Gospel lesson presents and includes it. It will, however, be a stench in the nostrils of the pope! But how shall I deal differently with him? The text says: "He that entereth not by the door into the fold of the sheep, but climbeth up some other way, the same is a thief and a robber (murderer)."

2. This verse has been explained as having reference to those who climb, by their presumption, into the best church livings through favor and wealth, recommendations or their own power, not obtaining them by regular appointment and authority. And at present the most pious jurists are punishing people for running to Rome after fees and benefices, or after ecclesiastical preferment and offices. This they call simony. The practice is truly deplorable, for much depends upon being regularly called and appointed. No one should step into the office and preach from his own presumption and without a commission from those having the authority. But under present conditions, if we should wait until we received a commission to preach and to administer the sacraments, we would never perform those offices as long as we live. For the bishops in our day press into their offices by force, and those who have the power of preferment are influenced by friendship and rank. But I pass this by, and will speak of the true office, into which no one forces his way (even though his devotion urge him) without being called by others having the authority.

3. True, we all have authority to preach, yea, we must preach God's name; we are commanded to do so. Peter says in his first Epistle, (2:9-10) "But ye are an elect race, a royal priesthood, a holy nation, a people for God's own possession, that ye may show forth the excellencies of him who called you out of darkness into his marvellous light: who in time past were no people, but now are the people of God: who had not obtained mercy, but now have obtained mercy." Nevertheless, Paul establishes order in 1 Cor. 14:40 and says: "In whatever you do among yourselves, let everything be done decently and in order." In a family there must be order. If all the heirs strive for lordship, anarchy will reign in the family. If, however, by common consent, one of the number is selected for the heirship, the others withdrawing, harmony will obtain. Likewise, in the matter of preaching we must make selection that order may be preserved...

Section II. Preachers of the Word to Preach Nothing but the Word.

4. So much for the call into the office. But Christ is not speaking of that here; for something more is required, namely, that no rival or supplementary doctrine be introduced, nor another word be taught than Christ has taught. Christ says in Mt. 23:2-4: "The scribes and the Pharisees sit on Moses' seat: all things therefore whatsoever they bid you, these do and observe: but do not ye after their works; for they say and do not. Yea, they bind heavy burdens too grievous to be borne, and lay them on men's shoulders; but they themselves will not move them with their finger." Although these of whom Christ here speaks were regularly appointed, yet they were thieves and murderers; for they taught variations from Christ's teaching. Christ reproves them in another place, in Matthew 15:3, where he holds up before them their traditions and tells them how, through their own inventions, they have transgressed the commandments

of God, yea, totally abolished them. We have also many prophets who were regularly appointed and still were misled, like Balaam, of whom we read in Num. 22; also Nathan, described in 2 Sam 7:3. Similarly many bishops have erred.

5. Here Christ says: He who would enter by the door must be ready to speak the Word concerning Christ and his word must center in Christ. Let it be called "coming" when one preaches aright; the approaching is spiritual, and through the Word—upon the ears of his hearers, the preacher comes at last into the sheepfold—the heart of believers. Christ says that the shepherd must enter by the door; that is, preach nothing but Christ, for Christ is the door into the sheepfold.

6. But where there are intruders, who make their own door, their own hole to crawl through, their own addition different from that which Christ taught, they are thieves. Of these Paul says to the Romans (16:17-18): "Now I beseech you, brethren, mark them that are causing the divisions and occasions of stumbling, contrary to the doctrine which ye learned: and turn away from them. For they that are such serve not our Lord Christ, but their own belly; and by their smooth and fair speech they beguile the hearts of the innocent." Paul does not speak of opposing or antagonistic doctrines, but of those placed beside the true doctrine; they are additions, making divisions. Paul calls it a rival doctrine, an addition, an occasion of stumbling, an offense and a byway, when one establishes the conscience upon his own goodness or deeds.

7. Now, the Gospel is sensitive, complete and pre-eminent: it must be intolerant of additions and rival teachings. The doctrine of earning entrance into heaven by virtue of fastings, prayers and penance is a branch road, which the Gospel will not tolerate. But our Church authorities endorse these things, hence they are thieves and murderers; for they do violence to our consciences, which is slaying and destroying the sheep. How is this accomplished? If only I am directed into a branch or parallel road, then my soul is turned from God upon that road, where I must perish. Thus this road is the cause of my death. The conscience and heart of man must be founded upon one single Word or they will come to grief. "All flesh is grass, and all the goodliness thereof is as the flower of the field" (Is 40:6).

8. The doctrines of men, however admirable, fall to the ground, and with them the conscience that has built upon them. There is no help nor remedy. But the Word of God is eternal and must endure forever; no devil can overthrow it. The foundation is laid upon which the conscience may be established forever. The words of men must perish and everything that cleaves to them. Those who enter not by the door—that is, those who do not speak the true and pure Word of God, without any addition—do not lay the right foundation; they destroy and torture and slaughter the sheep. Therefore, Christ says further in this Gospel: "But he that entereth in by the door is the shepherd of the sheep. To him the porter openeth; and the sheep hear his Voice."

Section III. A True Preacher Should First Use the Law Aright and Then Preach the Gospel.

9. The porter here is the preacher who rightly teaches the Law—shows that the Law exists and must reveal to us our helplessness; that the works of the Law do not help us, and yet they are insistent. He then opens to the shepherd, that is, to Christ the Lord, and lets him alone feed the sheep. For the office of the Law is at an end; it has accomplished its mission of revealing to the heart its sins until it is completely humbled. Then Christ comes and makes a lamb out of the sheep—feeds it with his Gospel and directs it how to regain cheer for the heart so hopelessly troubled and crushed by the Law.

10. The lamb then hears Christ's voice and follows it. It has the choicest of pastures, and knows the voice of the shepherd. But the voice of a stranger it never hears and never follows. Just as soon as one preaches to it about works, it is worried and its heart cannot receive the teaching with joy. It knows very well that nothing is accomplished by means of works; for one may do as much as he will, still he carries a heavy spirit and he thinks he has not done enough, nor done rightly. But when the Gospel comes—the voice of the shepherd—it says: God gave to the world his only Son, that all who believe on him should not perish, but have everlasting life. Then is the heart happy; it feeds upon these words and finds them good. The lamb has found its satisfying pasture; it wants none other. Yea, when it is given other pasture, it flees from it and will not feed therein. This pasture always attracts the sheep, and the sheep also find it. God says in the prophecy of Isaiah: "So shall my Word be that goeth forth out of my mouth: it shall not return unto me void, but it shall accomplish all in the things whereto, I sent it" (Is 55:11).

Section IV. The Hearers Have the Right to Examine and Judge a Sermon

"And he calleth his own sheep by name, and leadeth them out. When he hath put forth all his own, he goeth before them and the sheep follow him; for they know his voice. And a stranger will they not follow, but will flee from him; for they know not the voice of strangers."

11. In this text there are two thoughts worthy of note: the liberty of faith, and the power to judge. You know that our soul-murderers have proposed to us that what the councils and the learned doctors decide and decree, that we should accept, and not judge for ourselves whether it is right or not. They have become so certain of the infallibility of the councils and doctors that they have now established the edict, publicly seen, that if we do not accept what they say, we are put under the ban. Now, let us take a spear in hand and make a hole in their shield; yea, their resolutions shall be a spider's web. And you should, moreover, use upon them the spear which until now they have used upon us,

and hold before them its point.

12. Remember well that the sheep have to pass judgment upon that which is placed before them. They should say: We have Christ as our Lord and prefer his Word to the words of any man or to those of the angels of darkness. We want to examine and judge for ourselves whether the pope, the bishops and their followers do right or not. For Christ says here that the sheep judge and know which is the right voice and which is not. Now let them come along. Have they decreed anything? We will examine whether it is right, and according to our own judgment interpret that which is a private affair for each individual Christian, knowing that the authority to do this is not human, but divine. Even the real sheep flee from a stranger and hold to the voice of their shepherd.

13. Upon this authority., the Gospel knocks all the councils, all the papistic laws, to the ground, granting to us that we should receive nothing without judging it, that we have besides the power to judge, and that such judgment stands until the present day. The papists have taken from us the sword, so that we have not been able to repel any false doctrine, and, moreover, they have by force introduced false teachings among us. If now we take the sword from them they will be sorry. And we must truly take it, not by force, but by means of the Word, letting go all else that we have, saying: I am God's sheep, whose Word I wish to appropriate to myself. If you will give me that, I will acknowledge you to be a shepherd. If you, however, add another Gospel to this one, and do not give me the pure Gospel, then I will not consider you a shepherd, and will not listen to your voice; for the office of which you boast extends no farther than the Word goes. If we find one to be a shepherd, we should receive him as such: if he is not, we should remove him; for the sheep shall judge the voice of the shepherd. If he does not give us the right kind of pasture, we should bid farewell to such a shepherd, that is, to the bishop; for a hat of pearls and a staff of silver do not make a shepherd or a bishop, but rather does the office depend upon his care of the sheep and their pasture.

14. Now the papists object to judgment being passed upon any of their works; for this reason they have intruded and taken from us the sword which we might use for such a purpose. Also, they dictate that we must accept, without any right of judgment, whatever they propose. And it has almost come to such a pass that whenever the pope breathes they make an article of faith out of it, and they have proclaimed that the authorities have the right to pass such laws for their subjects as they desire, independent of the judgment of the latter. These conditions mean ruin to the Christians, so much so that a hundred thousand swords should be desired for one pope. This they know very well, and they cling hard to their laws. If they would permit unbiased judgment, their laws would be set aside and they would have to preach the pure Word; but such a course would reduce the size of their stomachs and the number of their horses.

15. Therefore, be ye aroused by this passage of Scripture to hew to pieces

and thrust through everything that is not in harmony with the Gospel, for it belongs to the sheep to judge, and not to the preachers. You have the authority and power to judge everything that is preached; that and nothing less. If we have not this power, then Christ vainly said to us in Mt. 7:15: "Beware of false prophets, who come to you in sheep's clothing, but inwardly are ravening wolves." We could not beware if we had not the power to judge, but were obliged to accept everything they said and preached.

V. Preachers Are to Force No One to Believe.

16. The second thought is, no one shall be forced to believe; for the sheep follow him whom they know and flee from strangers. Now, Christ's wish is that none be forced, but that they be permitted to follow from willing hearts and of their own desire; not out of fear, shame or strife. He would let the Word go forth and accomplish all. When their hearts are taken captive, then they will surely come of themselves. Faith does not go forth from the heart unless it has the Word of God.

17. Our noblemen are now mad and foolish in that they undertake to drive people to believe by means of force and the sword. Christ here wishes the sheep to come of themselves, from their knowledge of his voice. The body may be forced, as the pope, for example, has by his laws coerced people to go to confession and to the Lord's Supper, but the heart cannot be taken captive. Christ wants it to be free. Although he had power to coerce men, he wished to win them through his pleasing, loving preaching. Whoever lays hold of Christ's word follows after him and permits nothing to, tear him from it. The noblemen wish to drive the people to believe by means of the sword and fire; that is nonsense. Then let us see to it that we allow the pure Word of God to take its course, and afterward leave them free to follow, whom it has taken captive; yea, they will follow voluntarily.

18. By this I do not wish to abolish the civil sword; for the hand can hold it within its grasp so that it does no one any harm, but it holds it inactive. It must be retained because of wicked villains who have no regard at all for the Word; but the sword cannot force the heart and bring it to faith. In view of its inability, it must keep silent in matters of faith; here one must enter by the door, and preach the Word and make the heart free. Only in this way are men led to believe. These are the two expedients—for the pious and the wicked: the pious are to be drawn by the Word, and the wicked to be driven by the sword to observe order.

VI. The Marks of False Preachers.

19. Now, Christ interprets his own words. He says that he is the door to the sheep, but all the others who came before him, that is, those who were not sent by God as the prophets were, but came of themselves, uncommissioned, are thieves and murderers; they steal his honor from God and strangle human souls

by their false doctrines. But Christ is the door, and whoever enters by him will be saved, and will go in and out and find pasture. Here Christ speaks of the Christian liberty, which means that Christians are now free from the curse and the tyranny of the Law, and may keep the Law or not, according as they see that the love and need of their neighbor requires. This is what Paul did. When he was among the Jews, he kept the Law with the Jews; when among the gentiles, he kept it as they kept it, which he himself says in 1 Cor. 9:19-23:

"For though I was free from all men, I brought myself under bondage to all, that I might gain the more. And to the Jews I became as a Jew, that I might gain Jews; to them that are under the law, as under the law, not being myself under the law, that I might gain them that are under the law; to them that are without law, as without law, not being without law to God, but under law to Christ, that I might gain them that are without law. To the weak I became weak, that I might gain the weak: I am become all things to all men, that I may by all means save some. And I do all things for the gospel's sake, that I may be a joint partaker thereof."

20. That, the thieves and murderers, the false teachers and prophets, never do; they accomplish nothing but to steal, strangle and destroy the sheep. But Christ, the true and faithful shepherd, comes only that the sheep may have life and be fully satisfied. This is enough on today's Gospel for the present. We will conclude and pray God for grace rightly to lay hold of it and understand it.

The Twofold Use of the Law & Gospel: "Letter" & "Spirit"

Second Corinthians 3:4-11. 4 And such confidence have we through Christ to Godward: 5 not that we are sufficient of ourselves, to account anything as from ourselves; but our sufficiency is from God; 6 who also made us sufficient as ministers of a new covenant; not of the letter, but of the spirit: for the letter killeth, but the spirit giveth life. 7 But if the ministration of death, written, and engraven on stones, came with glory, so that the children of Israel could not look stedfastly upon the face of Moses for the glory of his face; which glory was passing away: 8 how shall not rather the ministration of the spirit be with glory? 9 For if the ministration of condemnation hath glory, much rather doth the ministration of righteousness exceed in glory. 10 For verily that which hath been made glorious hath not been made glorious in this respect, by reason of the glory that surpasseth. 11 For if that which passeth away was with glory, much more that which remaineth is in glory.

Gospel Transcends Law

1. This epistle lesson sounds altogether strange and wonderful to individuals unaccustomed to Scripture language, particularly to that of Paul. To the inexperienced ear and heart it is not intelligible. In popedom thus far it has remained quite unapprehended, although reading of the words has been practiced.

2. That we may understand it, we must first get an idea of Paul's theme. Briefly, he would oppose the vain boasting of false apostles and preachers concerning their possession of the spirit and their peculiar skill and gifts, by praising and glorifying the office of a preacher of the Gospel with which he is intrusted. For he found that, especially in the Church at Corinth, which he had converted by the words of his own lips and brought to faith in Christ, soon after his departure the devil introduced his heresies whereby the people were turned from the truth and betrayed into other ways. Since it became his duty to make an attack upon such heresies, he devoted both his epistles to the purpose of keeping the Corinthians in the right way, so that they might retain the pure doctrine received from him, and beware of false spirits. The main thing which moved him to write this second epistle was his desire to emphasize to them his

apostolic office of a preacher of the Gospel, in order to put to shame the glory of those other teachers—the glory they boasted with many words and great pretense.

3. He starts in on this theme just before he reaches our text. And this is how it is he comes to speak in high terms of praise of the ministration of the Gospel and to contrast and compare the twofold ministration or message which may be proclaimed in the Church, provided, of course, that God's Word is to be preached and not the nonsense of human falsehood and the doctrine of the devil. One is that of the Old Testament, the other of the New; in other words, the office of Moses, or the Law, and the office of the Gospel of Christ. He contrasts the glory and power of the latter with those of the former, which, it is true, is also the Word of God. In this manner he endeavors to defeat the teachings and pretensions of those seductive spirits who, as he but lately foretold, pervert God"s Word, in that they greatly extol the Law of God, yet at best do not teach its right use, but, instead of making it tributary to faith in Christ, misuse it to teach work-righteousness.

4. Since the words before us are in reality a continuation of those with which the chapter opens, the latter must be considered in this connection. We read:

"Are we beginning again to commend ourselves? or need we, as do some, epistles of commendation to you or from you? Ye are our epistle, written in our hearts, known and read of all men; being made manifest that ye are an epistle of Christ, ministered by us, written not with ink, but with the Spirit of the living God; not in tables of stone, but in tables that are hearts of flesh."

"We, my fellow-apostles and co-laborers and I," he says, "do not ask for letters and seals from others commending us to you, or from you commending us to others, in order to seduce people after gaining their good will in your church and in others as well. Such is the practice of the false apostles, and many even now present letters and certificates from honest preachers and Churches, and make them the means whereby their unrighteous plotting may be received in good faith. Such letters, thank God, we stand not in need of, and you need not fear we shall use such means of deception. For you are yourselves the letter we have written and wherein we may pride ourselves and which we present everywhere. For it is a matter of common knowledge that you have been taught by us, and brought to Christ through our ministry."

Paul's Converts Living Epistles

5. Inasmuch as his activity among them is his testimonial, and they themselves are aware that through his ministerial office he has constituted them a church, he calls them an epistle written by himself; not with ink and in paragraphs, not on paper or wood, nor engraved upon hard rock as the Ten Commandments written upon tables of stone, which Moses placed before the people, but written by the Holy Spirit upon fleshly tables—hearts of tender flesh. The Spirit is the ink or the inscription, yes, even the writer himself; but

the pencil or pen and the hand of the writer is the ministry of Paul.

6. This figure of a written epistle is, however, in accord with Scripture usage. Moses commands (Deut 6:6-9; 11, 18) that the Israelites write the Ten Commandments in all places where they walked or stood upon the posts of their houses, and upon their gates, and ever have them before their eyes and in their hearts. Again (Prov 7:2-3), Solomon says: "Keep my commandments and...my law as the apple of thine eye. Bind them upon thy fingers; write them upon the tablet of thy heart." He speaks as a father to his child when giving the child an earnest charge to remember a certain thing—"Dear child, remember this; forget it not; keep it in thy heart." Likewise, God says in the book of Jeremiah the prophet (ch. 31, 33), "I will put my law in their inward parts, and in their heart will I write it." Here man's heart is represented as a sheet, or slate, or page, whereon is written the preached Word; for the heart is to receive and securely keep the Word. In this sense Paul says: "We have, by our ministry, written a booklet or letter upon your heart, which witnesses that you believe in God the Father, Son and Holy Ghost and have the assurance that through Christ you are redeemed and saved. This testimony is what is written on your heart. The letters are not characters traced with ink or crayon, but the living thoughts, the fire and force of the heart.

7. Note further, that it is his ministry to which Paul ascribes the preparation of their heart thereon and the inscription which constitutes them "living epistles of Christ." He contrasts his ministry with the blind fancies of those fanatics who seek to receive, and dream of having, the Holy Spirit without the oral word; who, perchance, creep into a corner and grasp the Spirit through dreams, directing the people away from the preached Word and visible ministry. But Paul says that the Spirit, through his preaching, has wrought in the hearts of his Corinthians, to the end that Christ lives and is mighty in them. After such statement he bursts into praise of the ministerial office, comparing the message, or preaching, of Moses with that of himself and the apostles. He says:

"Such confidence have we through Christ to Godward: not that we are sufficient of ourselves, to account anything as from ourselves; but our sufficiency is from God

True Preachers Commissioned by God

8. These words are blows and thrusts for the false apostles and preachers. Paul is mortal enemy to the blockheads who make great boast, pretending to what they do not possess and to what they cannot do; who boast of having the Spirit in great measure; who are ready to counsel and aid the whole world; who pride themselves on the ability to invent something new. It is to be a surpassingly precious and heavenly thing they are to spin out of their heads, as the dreams of pope and monks have been in time past.

"We do not so," says Paul. "We rely not upon ourselves or our wisdom and ability. We preach not what we have ourselves invented. But this is our boast and trust in Christ before God, that we have made of you a divine epistle; have written upon your hearts, not our thoughts, but the Word of God. We are not, however, glorifying our own power, but the works and the power of him who has called and equipped us for such an office; from whom proceeds all you have heard and believed.

9. It is a glory which every preacher may claim, to be able to say with full confidence of heart: "This trust have I toward God in Christ, that what I teach and preach is truly the Word of God." Likewise, when he performs other official duties in the Church—baptizes a child, absolves and comforts a sinner—it must be done in the same firm conviction that such is the command of Christ.

10. He who would teach and exercise authority in the Church without this glory, "it is profitable for him," as Christ says (Mt. 18:6), "that a great millstone should be hanged about his neck, and that he should be sunk in the depths of the sea." For the devil's lies he preaches, and death is what he effects. Our Papists, in time past, after much and long-continued teaching, after many inventions and works whereby they hoped to be saved, nevertheless always doubted in heart and mind whether or no they had pleased God. The teaching and works of all heretics and seditious spirits certainly do not bespeak for them trust in Christ; their own glory is the object of their teaching, and the homage and praise of the people is the goal of their desire. "Not that we are sufficient of ourselves, to account anything as from ourselves."

11. As said before, this is spoken in denunciation of the false spirits who believe that by reason of eminent equipment of special creation and election, they are called to come to the rescue of the people, expecting wonders from whatever they say and do.

Human Doctrine No Place in the Church

12. Now, we know ourselves to be of the same clay whereof they are made; indeed, we perhaps have the greater call from God: yet we cannot boast of being capable of ourselves to advise or aid men. We cannot even originate an idea calculated to give help. And when it comes to the knowledge of how one may stand before God and attain to eternal life, that is truly not to be achieved by our work or power, nor to originate in our brain. In other things, those pertaining to this temporal life, you may glory in what You know, you may advance the teachings of reason, you may invent ideas of your own; for example: how to make shoes or clothes, how to govern a household, how to manage a herd. In such things exercise your mind to the best of your ability. Cloth or leather of this sort will permit itself to be stretched and cut according to the good pleasure of the tailor or shoemaker. But in spiritual matters, human reasoning certainly is not in order; other intelligence, other skill and power, are requisite here—something to be granted by God himself and revealed through his Word.

13. What mortal has ever discovered or fathomed the truth that the three

persons in the eternal divine essence are one God; that the second person, the Son of God, was obliged to become man, born of a virgin; and that no way of life could be opened for us, save through his crucifixion? Such truth never would have been heard nor preached, would never in all eternity have been published, learned and believed, had not God himself revealed it.

14. For this season they are blind fools of first magnitude and dangerous characters who would boast of their grand performances, and think that the people are served when they preach their own fancies and inventions. It has been the practice in the Church for anyone to introduce any teaching he saw fit; for example, the monks and priests have daily produced new saints, pilgrimages, special prayers, works and sacrifices in the effort to blot out sin, redeem souls from purgatory, and so on. They who make up things of this kind are not such as put their trust in God through Christ, but rather such as defy God and Christ. Into the hearts of men, where Christ alone should be, they shove the filth and write the lies of the devil. Yet they think themselves, and themselves only, qualified for all essential teaching and work, self-grown doctors that they are, saints all-powerful without the help of God and Christ.

"But our sufficiency is from God."

15. Of ourselves—in our own wisdom and strength—we cannot effect, discover nor teach any counsel or help for man, whether for ourselves or others. Any good work we perform among you, any doctrine we write upon your heart that is God's own work. He puts into our heart and mouth what we should say, and impresses it upon your heart through the Holy Spirit. Therefore, we cannot ascribe to ourselves any honor therein, cannot seek our own glory as the self-instructed and proud spirits do; we must give to God alone the honor, and must glory in the fact that by his grace and power he works in you unto Salvation, through the office committed unto us.

16. Now, Paul's thought here is that nothing should be taught and practiced in the Church but what is unquestionably God's Word. It will not do to introduce or perform anything whatever upon the strength of man's judgment. Man's achievements, man's reasoning and power, are of no avail save in so far as they come from God. As Peter says in his first epistle (ch. 4:11): "If any man speaketh, speaking as it were oracles of God; if any man ministereth, ministering as of the strength which God supplieth." In short, let him who would be wise, who would boast of great skill, talents and power, confine himself to things other than spiritual; with respect to spiritual matters, let him keep his place and refrain from boasting and pretense. For it is of no moment that men observe your greatness and ability; the important thing is that poor souls may rest assured of being presented with God's Word and works, whereby they may be saved.

"Who also made us sufficient as ministers of a new covenant; not of the letter, but of the spirit: for the letter killeth, but the spirit giveth life."

The New Covenant

17. Paul here proceeds to exalt the office and power of the Gospel over the glorying of the false apostles, and to elevate the power of the Word above that of all other doctrine, even of the Law of God. Truly we are not sufficient of ourselves and have nothing to boast of so far as human activity is considered. For that is without merit or power, however strenuous the effort may be to fulfil God's Law. We have, however, something infinitely better to boast of, something not grounded in our own activity: by God we have been made sufficient for a noble ministry, termed the ministry "of a New Covenant." This ministry is not only exalted far above any teaching to be evolved by human wisdom, skill and power, but is more glorious than the ministry termed the "Old Covenant," which in time past was delivered to the Jews through Moses. While this ministry clings, in common with other doctrine, to the Word given by revelation, it is the agency whereby the Holy Spirit works in the heart. Therefore, Paul says it is not a ministration of the letter, but ""of the spirit."

"Spirit" & "Letter"

18. This passage relative to spirit and letter has in the past been wholly strange language to us. Indeed, to such extent has man's nonsensical interpretation perverted and weakened it that I, through a learned doctor of the holy Scriptures, failed to understand it altogether, and I could find no one to teach me. And to this day it is unintelligible to all popedom. In fact, even the old teachers—Origen, Jerome and others—have not caught Paul's thought. And no wonder, truly! For it is essentially a doctrine far beyond the power of man's intelligence to comprehend. When human reason meddles with it, it becomes perplexed. The doctrine is wholly unintelligible to it, for human thought goes no farther than the Law and the Ten Commandments. Laying hold upon these it confines itself to them. It does not attempt to do more, being governed by the principle that unto him who fulfils the demands of the Law, or commandments, God is gracious. Reason knows nothing about the wretchedness of depraved nature. It does not recognize the fact that no man is able to keep God's commandments; that all are under sin and condemnation; and that the only way whereby help could be received was for God to give his Son for the world, ordaining another ministration, one through which grace and reconciliation might be proclaimed to us. Now, he who does not understand the sublime subject of which Paul speaks cannot but miss the true meaning of his words. How much more did we invite this fate when we threw the Scriptures and Saint Paul's epistles under the bench, and, like swine in husks, wallowed in man's nonsense! Therefore, we must submit to correction and learn to understand the apostle's utterance aright.

19. "Letter" and "spirit" have been understood to mean, according to Origen and Jerome, the obvious sense of the written word. St. Augustine, it must be admitted, has gotten an inkling of the truth. Now, the position of the former

teachers would perhaps not be quite incorrect did they correctly explain the words. By "literary sense" they signify the meaning of a Scripture narrative according to the ordinary interpretation of the words. By "spiritual sense" they signify the secondary, hidden sense found in the words.

For instance: The Scripture narrative in Genesis third records how the serpent persuaded the woman to eat of the forbidden fruit and to give to her husband, who also ate. This narrative in its simplest meaning represents what they understand by "letter." "Spirit," however, they understand to mean the spiritual interpretation, which is thus: The serpent signifies the evil temptation which lures to sin. The woman represents the sensual state, or the sphere in which such enticements and temptations make themselves felt. Adam, the man, stands for reason, which is called man's highest endowment. Now, when reason does not yield to the allurements of external sense, all is well; but when it permits itself to waver and consent, the fall has taken place.

20. Origen was the first to trifle thus with the holy Scriptures, and many others followed, until now it is thought to be the sign of great cleverness for the Church to be filled with such quibblings. The aim is to imitate Paul, who (Gal 4;22-24) figuratively interprets the story of Abraham's two sons, the one by the free woman, or the mistress of the house, and the other by the hand-maid. The two women, Paul says, represent the two covenants: one covenant makes only bondservants, which is just what he in our text terms the ministration of the letter; the other leads to liberty, or, as he says here, the ministration of the spirit, which gives life. And the two sons are the two peoples, one of which does not go farther than the Law, while the other accepts in faith the Gospel.

True, this is an interpretation not directly suggested by the narrative and the text. Paul himself calls it an allegory; that is, a mystic narrative, or a story with a hidden meaning. But he does not say that the literal text is necessarily the letter that killeth, and the allegory, or hidden meaning, the spirit. But the false teachers assert of all Scripture that the text, or record itself, is but a dead "letter," its interpretation being "the spirit." Yet they have not pushed interpretation farther than the teaching of the Law; and it is precisely the Law which Paul means when he speaks of "the letter."

21. Paul employs the word "letter" in such contemptuous sense in reference to the Law—though the Law is, nevertheless, the Word of God—when he compares it with the ministry of the Gospel. The letter is to him the doctrine of the Ten Commandments, which teach how we should obey God, honor parents, love our neighbor, and so on—the very best doctrine to be found in all books, sermons and schools.

The word "letter" is to the apostle Paul everything which may take the form of doctrine, of literary arrangement, of record, so long as it remains something spoken or written. Also thoughts which may be pictured or expressed by word or writing, but it is not that which is written in the heart, to become its life. "Letter" is the whole Law of Moses, or the Ten Commandments, though the supreme authority of such teaching is not denied. It matters not whether you hear them, read them, or reproduce them mentally. For instance, when I sit down to meditate upon the first commandment: "Thou shalt have no other gods before me," or the second, or the third, and so forth, I have something which I can read, write, discuss, and aim to fulfil with all my might. The process is quite similar when the emperor or prince gives a command and says: "This you shall do, that you shall eschew." This is what the apostle calls "the letter," or, as we have called it on another occasion, the written sense.

22. Now, as opposed to "the letter," there is another doctrine or message, which he terms the "ministration of a New Covenant" and "of the Spirit." This doctrine does not teach what works are required of man, for that man has already heard; but it makes known to him what God would do for him and bestow upon him, indeed what he has already done: he has given his Son Christ for us; because, for our disobedience to the Law, which no man fulfils, we were under God's wrath and condemnation. Christ made satisfaction for our sins, effected a reconciliation with God and gave to us his own righteousness. Nothing is said in this ministration of man's deeds; it tells rather of the works of Christ, who is unique in that he was born of a virgin, died for sin and rose from the dead, something no other man has been able to do. This doctrine is revealed through none but the Holy Spirit, and none other confers the Holy Spirit. The Holy Spirit works in the hearts of them who hear and accept the doctrine. Therefore, this ministration is termed a ministration "of the Spirit."

23. The apostle employs the words "letter" and "spirit," to contrast the two doctrines; to emphasize his office and show its advantage over all others, however eminent the teachers whom they boast, and however great the spiritual unction which they vaunt. It is of design that he does not term the two dispensations "Law" and "Gospel," but names them according to the respective effects produced. He honors the Gospel with a superior term—"ministration of the spirit." Of the Law, on the contrary, he speaks almost contemptuously, as if he would not honor it with the title of God's commandment, which in reality it is, according to his own admission later on that its deliverance to Moses and its injunction upon the children of Israel was an occasion of surpassing glory.

24. Why does Paul choose this method? Is it right for one to despise or dishonor God's Law? Is not a chaste and honorable life a matter of beauty and godliness? Such facts, it may be contended, are implanted by God in reason itself, and all books teach them; they are the governing force in the world. I reply: Paul's chief concern is to defeat the vainglory and pretensions of false preachers, and to teach them the right conception and appreciation of the Gospel which he proclaimed. What Paul means is this: When the Jews vaunt their Law of Moses, which was received as Law from God and recorded upon two tables of stone; when they vaunt their learned and saintly preachers of the Law and its exponents, and hold their deeds and manner of life up to admiration, what is all that compared to the Gospel message? The claim may

be well made: a fine sermon, a splendid exposition; but, after all, nothing more comes of it than precepts, expositions, written comments. The precept, "Thou shalt love the Lord thy God with all thy heart, and thy neighbor as thyself," remains a mere array of words. When much time and effort have been spent in conforming one's life to it, nothing has been accomplished. You have pods without peas, husks without kernels.

25. For it is impossible to keep the Law without Christ, though man may, for the sake of honor or property, or from fear of punishment, feign outward holiness. The heart which does not discern God's grace in Christ cannot turn to God nor trust in him; it cannot love his commandments and delight in them, but rather resists them. For nature rebels at compulsion. No man likes to be a captive in chains. One does not voluntarily bow to the rod of punishment or submit to the executioner's sword; rather, because of these things, his anger against the Law is but increased, and he ever thinks: "Would that I might unhindered steal, rob, hoard, gratify my lust, and so on!" And when restrained by force, he would there were no Law and no God. And this is the case where conduct shows some effects of discipline, in that the outer man has been subjected to the teaching of the Law.

26. But in a far more appalling degree does inward rebellion ensue when the heart feels the full force of the Law; when, standing before God's judgment, it feels the sentence of condemnation; as we shall presently hear, for the apostle says "the letter killeth." Then the truly hard knots appear. Human nature fumes and rages against the Law; offenses appear in the heart, the fruit of hate and enmity against the Law; and presently human nature flees before God and is incensed at God's judgment. It begins to question the equity of his dealings, to ask if he is a just God. Influenced by such thoughts, it falls ever deeper into doubt, it murmurs and chafes, until finally, unless the Gospel comes to the rescue, it utterly despairs, as did Judas, and Saul, and perhaps pass out of this life with God and creation. This is what Paul means when he says (Rom 7:8-9) that the Law works sin in the heart of man, and sin works death, or kills.

27. You see, then, why the Law is called "the letter": though noble doctrine, it remains on the surface; it does not enter the heart as a vital force which begets obedience. Such is the baseness of human nature, it will not and cannot conform to the Law; and so corrupt is mankind, there is no individual who does not violate all God's commandments in spite of daily hearing the preached Word and having held up to view God's wrath and eternal condemnation. Indeed, the harder pressed man is, the more furiously he storms against the Law.

28. The substance of the matter is this: When all the commandments have been put together, when their message receives every particle of praise to which it is entitled, it is still a mere letter. That is, teaching not put into practice. By "letter" is signified all manner of law, doctrine and message, which goes no farther than the oral or written word, which consists only of the powerless letter. To illustrate: A law promulgated by a prince or the authorities of a city,

if not enforced, remains merely an open letter, which makes a demand indeed, but ineffectually. Similarly, God's Law, although a teaching of supreme authority and the eternal will of God, must suffer itself to become a mere empty letter or husk. Without a quickening heart, and devoid of fruit, the Law is powerless to effect life and salvation. It may well be called a veritable table of omissions (Lass-tafel); that is, it is a written enumeration, not of duties performed but of duties cast aside. In the languages of the world, it is a royal edict which remains unobserved and unperformed. In this light St. Augustine understood the Law. He says, commenting on Psalm 17, "What is Law without grace but a letter without spirit?" Human nature, without the aid of Christ and his grace, cannot keep it.

29. Again, Paul in terming the Gospel a "ministration of the spirit" would call attention to its power to produce in the hearts of men an effect wholly different from that of the Law: it is accompanied by the Holy Spirit and it creates a new heart. Man, driven into fear and anxiety by the preaching of the Law, hears this Gospel message, which, instead of reminding him of God's demands, tells him what God has done for him. It points not to man's works, but to the works of Christ, and bids him confidently believe that for the sake of his Son God will forgive his sins and accept him as his child. And this message, when received in faith, immediately cheers and comforts the heart. The heart will
no longer flee from God; rather it turns to him. Finding grace with God and experiencing his mercy, the heart feels drawn to him. It commences to call upon him and to treat and revere him as its beloved God. In proportion as such faith and solace grow, also love for the commandments will grow and obedience to them will be man's delight. Therefore, God would have his Gospel message urged unceasingly as the means of awakening man's heart to discern his state and recall the great grace and lovingkindness of God, with the result that the power of the Holy Spirit is increased constantly. Note, no influence of the Law, no work of man is present here. The force is a new and heavenly one—the power of the Holy Spirit. He impresses upon the heart Christ and his works, making of it a true book which does not consist in the tracery of mere letters and words, but in true life and action.

30. God promised of old, in Joel 2:28 and other passages, to give the Spirit through the new message, the Gospel. And he has verified his promise by public manifestations in connection with the preaching of that Gospel, as on the day of Pentecost and again later. When the apostles, Peter and others, began to preach, the Holy Spirit descended visibly from heaven upon their hearts. Acts 8:17; 10:44. Up to that time, throughout the period the Law was preached, no one had heard or seen such manifestation. The fact could not but be grasped that this was a vastly different message from that of the Law when such mighty results followed in its train. And yet its substance was no more than what Paul declared (Acts 13:38-39): "Through this man is proclaimed unto you remission

of sins: and by him every one that believeth is justified from all things, from which ye could not be justified by the law of Moses."

31. In this teaching you see no more the empty letters, the valueless husks or shells of the Law, which unceasingly enjoins., "This thou shalt do and observe," and ever in vain. You see instead the true kernel and power which confers Christ and the fullness of His Spirit. In consequence, men heartily believe the message of the Gospel and enjoy its riches. They are accounted as having fulfilled the Ten Commandments. John says (Jn 1:16-17): "Of his fullness we all received, and grace for grace. For the Law was given through Moses; grace and truth came through Jesus Christ." John's thought is: The Law has indeed been given by Moses, but what avails that fact? To be sure, it is a noble doctrine and portrays a beautiful and instructive picture of man's duty to God and all mankind; it is really excellent as to the letter. Yet it remains empty; it does not enter into the heart. Therefore it is called "law," nor can it become aught else, so long as nothing more is given.

Christ Supersedes Moses

Before there can be fulfilment, another than Moses must come, bringing another doctrine. Instead of a law enjoined, there must be grace and truth revealed. For to enjoin a command and to embody the truth are two different things; just as teaching and doing differ. Moses, it is true, teaches the doctrine of the Law, so far as exposition is concerned, but he can neither fulfil it himself nor give others the ability to do so. That it might be fulfilled, God's Son had to come with his fullness; he has fulfilled the Law for himself and it is he who communicates to our empty heart the power to attain to the same fullness.

This becomes possible when we receive grace for grace, that is, when we come to the enjoyment of Christ, and for the sake of him who enjoys with God fullness of grace, although our own obedience to the Law is still imperfect. Being possessed of solace and grace, we receive by his power the Holy Spirit also, so that, instead of harboring mere empty letters within us, we come to the truth and begin to fulfil God's Law, in such a way, however, that we draw from his fullness and drink from that as a fountain.

Christ the Source of Life Greater than Adam the Source of Death

32. Paul gives us the same thought in Romans 5:17-18, where he compares Adam and Christ. Adam, he says, by his disobedience in Paradise, became the source of sin and death in the world; by the sin of this one man, condemnation passed upon all men. But on the other hand, Christ, by his obedience and righteousness, has become for us the abundant source wherefrom all may obtain righteousness and the power of obedience. And with respect to the latter source, it is far richer and more abundant than the former. While by the single

sin of one man, sin and death passed upon all men, to wax still more powerful with the advent of the Law, of such surpassing strength and greatness, on the other hand, is the grace and bounty which we have in Christ that it not only washes away the particular sin of the one man Adam, which, until Christ came, overwhelmed all men in death, but overwhelms and blots out all sin whatever. Thus they who receive his fullness of grace and bounty unto righteousness are, according to Paul, lords of life through Jesus Christ alone.

The Law Ineffectual

33. You see now how the two messages differ, and why Paul exalts the one, the preaching of the Gospel, and calls it a "ministration of the spirit," but terms the other, the Law, a mere empty "letter." His object is to humble the pride of the false apostles and preachers which they felt in their Judaism and the law of Moses, telling the people with bold pretensions: "Beloved, let Paul preach what he will, he cannot overthrow Moses, who on Mount Sinai received the Law, God's irrevocable command, obedience to which is ever the only way to salvation."

34. Similarly today, Papists, Anabaptists and other sects make outcry: "What mean you by preaching so much about faith and Christ? Are the people thereby made better? Surely works are essential." Arguments of this character have indeed a semblance of merit, but, when examined by the light of truth, are mere empty, worthless twaddle. For if deeds, or works, are to be considered, there are the Ten Commandments; we teach and practice these as well as they. The Commandments would answer the purpose indeed—if one could preach them so effectively as to compel their fulfilment. But the question is, whether what is preached is also practiced. Is there something more than were words—or letters, as Paul says? Do the words result in life and spirit? This message we have in common; unquestionably, one must teach the Ten Commandments, and, what is more, live them. But we charge that they are not observed. Therefore something else is requisite in order to render obedience to them possible. When Moses and the Law are made to say: "You should do thus; God demands this of you," what does it profit? Ay, beloved Moses, I hear that plainly, and it is certainly a righteous command; but pray tell me whence shall I obtain ability to do what, alas, I never have done nor can do? It is not easy to spend money from an empty pocket, or to drink from an empty can. If I am to pay my debt, or to quench my thirst, tell me how first to fill pocket or can. But upon this point such prattlers are silent; they but continue to drive and plague with the Law, let the people stick to their sins, and make merry of them to their own hurt.

35. In this light Paul here portrays the false apostles and like pernicious schismatics, who make great boasts of having a clearer understanding and of knowing much better what to teach than is the case with true preachers of the Gospel. And when they do their very best, when they pretend great things, and

do wonders with their preaching, there is naught but the mere empty "letter." Indeed, their message falls far short of Moses. Moses was a noble preacher, truly, and wrought greater things than any of them may do. Nevertheless, the doctrine of the Law could do no more than remain a letter, an Old Testament, and God had to ordain a different doctrine, a New Testament, which should impart the "spirit."

"It is the letter," says Paul, "which we preach. If any glorying is to be done, we can glory in better things and make the defiant plea that they are not the only teachers of what ought to be done, incapable as they are of carrying out their own precepts. We give direction and power as to performing and living those precepts. For this reason our message is not called the Old Testament, or the message of the dead letter, but that of the New Testament and of the living Spirit."

36. No seditious spirit, it is certain, ever carries out its own precepts, nor will he ever be capable of doing so, though he may loudly boast the Spirit alone as his guide. Of this fact you may rest assured. For such individuals know nothing more than the doctrine of works—nor can they rise higher and point you to anything else. They may indeed speak of Christ, but it is only to hold him up as an example of patience in suffering. In short, there can be no New Testament preached if the doctrine of faith in Christ be left out; the spirit cannot enter into the heart, but all teaching, endeavor, reflection, works and power remain mere "letters," devoid of grace, truth, and life. Without Christ the heart remains unchanged and unrenewed. It has no more power to fulfil the Law than the book in which the Ten Commandments are written, or the stones upon which engraved. "For the letter killeth, but the spirit giveth life."

37. Here is yet stronger condemnation of the glory of the doctrine of the Law; yet higher exaltation of the Gospel ministry. Is the apostle overbold in that he dares thus to assail the Law and say: "The Law is not only a lifeless letter, but qualified merely to kill"? Surely that is not calling the Law a good and profitable message, but one altogether harmful. Who, unless he would be a cursed heretic in the eyes of the world and invite execution as a blasphemer, would dare to speak thus, except Paul himself? Even Paul must praise the Law, which is God's command, declaring it good and not to be despised nor in any way modified, but to be confirmed and fulfilled so completely, as Christ says (Mt 5:18), that not a tittle of it shall pass away. How, then, does Paul come to speak so disparagingly, even abusively, of the Law, actually presenting it as veritable death and poison? Well, his is a sublime doctrine, one that reason does not understand. The world, particularly they Who would be called holy and godly, cannot tolerate it at all; for it amounts to nothing short of pronouncing all our works, however precious, mere death and poison.

38. Paul's purpose is to bring about the complete overthrow of the boast of the false teachers and hypocrites, and to reveal the weakness of their doctrine, showing how little it effects even at its best, since it offers only the Law, Christ

remaining unproclaimed and unknown. They say in terms of vainglorious eloquence that if a man diligently keep the commandments and do many good works, he shall be saved. But theirs are only vain words, a pernicious doctrine. This fact is eventually learned by him who, having heard no other doctrine, trusts in their false one. He finds out that it holds neither comfort nor power of life, but only doubt and anxiety, followed by death and destruction.

Terrors of the Law

39. When man, conscious of his failure to keep God's command, is constantly urged by the Law to make payment of his debt and confronted with nothing but the terrible wrath of God and eternal condemnation, he cannot but sink into despair over his sins. Such is the inevitable consequence where the Law alone is taught with a view to attaining heaven thereby. The vanity of such trust in works is illustrated in the case of the noted hermit mentioned in Vitae Patrum. (Lives of the Fathers). For over seventy years this hermit had led a life of utmost austerity, and had many followers. When the hour of death came he began to tremble, and for three days was in a state of agony. His disciples came to comfort him, exhorting him to die in peace since he had led so holy a life. But he replied: "Alas, I truly have all my life served Christ and lived austerely; but God's judgment greatly differs from that of men."

40. Note, this worthy man, despite the holiness of his life, has no acquaintance with any article but that of the divine judgment according to the Law. He knows not the comfort of Christ's Gospel. After a long life spent in the attempt to keep God's commandments and secure salvation, the Law now slays him through his own works. He is compelled to exclaim: "Alas, who knows how God will look upon my efforts? Who may stand before him?" That means, to forfeit heaven through the verdict of his own conscience. The work he has wrought and his holiness of life avail nothing. They merely push him deeper into death, since he is without the solace of the Gospel, while others, such as the thief on the cross and the publican, grasp the comfort of the Gospel, the forgiveness of sins in Christ. Thus sin is conquered; they escape the sentence of the Law, and pass through death into life eternal.

Efficacy of the Gospel

41. Now the meaning of the contrasting clause, "the spirit giveth life," becomes clear. The reference is to naught else but the holy Gospel, a message of healing and salvation; a precious, comforting word. It comforts and refreshes the sad heart. It wrests it out of the jaws of death and hell, as it were, and transports it to the certain hope of eternal life, through faith in Christ. When the last hour comes to the believer, and death and God's judgment appear before his eyes, he does not base his comfort upon his works. Even though he may have lived the holiest life possible, he says with Paul (1 Cor. 4:4): "I know nothing against myself, yet am I not hereby justified."

42. These words imply being ill pleased with self, with the whole life, indeed, even the putting to death of self. Though the heart says, "By my works I am neither made righteous nor saved," which is practically admitting oneself to be worthy of death and condemnation, the Spirit extricates from despair, through the Gospel faith, which confesses, as did St. Bernard in the hour of death: "Dear Lord Jesus, I am aware that my life at its best has been but worthy of condemnation, but I trust in the fact that thou hast died for me and hast sprinkled me with blood from thy holy wounds. For I have been baptized in thy name and have given heed to thy Word whereby thou hast called me, awarded me grace and life, and bidden me believe. In this assurance will I pass out of life; not in uncertainty and anxiety, thinking, 'Who knows what sentence God in heaven will pass upon me?'"

The Christian must not utter such a question. The sentence against his life and works has long since been passed by the Law. Therefore, he must confess himself guilty and condemned. But he lives by the gracious judgment of God declared from heaven, whereby the sentence of the Law is overruled and reversed. It is this: "He that believeth on the Son hath eternal life" (Jn. 3:36).

43. When the consolation of the Gospel has once been received and it has wrested the heart from death and the terrors of hell, the Spirit's influence is felt. By its power God's Law begins to live in man's heart; he loves it, delights in it and enters upon its fulfilment. Thus eternal life begins here, being continued forever and perfected in the life to come.

44. Now you see how much more glorious, how much better, is the doctrine of the apostles—the New Testament—than the doctrine of those who preach merely great works and holiness without Christ. We should see in this fact an incentive to hear the Gospel with gladness. We ought joyfully to thank God for it when we learn how it has power to bring to men life and eternal salvation, and when it gives us assurance that the Holy Spirit accompanies it and is imparted to believers.

"But if the ministration of death, written, and engraven on stones, came with glory, so that the children of Israel could not look stedfastly upon the face of Moses for the glory of his face; which glory was passing away: how shall not rather the ministration of the Spirit be with glory? For if the ministration of condemnation hath glory, much rather doth the ministration of righteousness exceed in glory."

Glory of the Gospel

45. Paul is in an ecstasy of delight, and his heart overflows in words of praise for the Gospel. Again he handles the Law severely, calling it a ministration, or doctrine, of death and condemnation. What term significant of greater abomination could he apply to God's Law than to call it a doctrine of death and hell? And again (Gal 2:17), he calls it a "minister (or preacher) of sin;" and (Gal 3:10) the message which proclaims a curse, saying, "As many as are

of the works of the law are under a curse." Absolute, then, is the conclusion that Law and works are powerless to justify before God; for how can a doctrine proclaiming only sin, death and condemnation justify and save?

46. Paul is compelled to speak thus, as we said above because of the infamous presumption of both teachers and pupils, in that they permit flesh and blood to coquet with the Law, and make their own works which they bring before God their boast. Yet, nothing is effected but self-deception and destruction. For, when the Law is viewed in its true light, when its "glory," as Paul has it, is revealed, it is found to do nothing more than to kill man and sink him into condemnation.

47. Therefore, the Christian will do well to learn this text of Paul and have an armor against the boasting of false teachers, and the torments and trials of the devil when he urges the Law and induces men to seek righteousness in their own works, tormenting their heart with the thought that salvation is dependent upon the achievements of the individual. The Christian will do well to learn this text, I say, so that in such conflicts he may take the devil's own sword, saying: "Why dost thou annoy me with talk of the Law and my works? What is the Law after all, however much you may preach it to me, but that which makes me feel the weight of sin, death and condemnation? Why should I seek therein righteousness before God?"

48. When Paul speaks of the "glory of the Law," of which the Jewish teachers of work-righteousness boast, he has reference to the things narrated in the twentieth and thirtyfourth chapters of Exodus—how, when the Law was given, God descended in majesty and glory from heaven, and there were thunderings and lightnings, and the mountain was encircled with fire; and how when Moses returned from the Mountain, bringing the Law, his face shone with a glory so dazzling that the people could not look upon his face and he was obliged to veil it.

49. Turning their glory against them, Paul says: "Truly, we do not deny the glory; splendor and majesty were there: but what does such glory do but compel souls to flee before God, and drive into death and hell? We believers, however, boast another glory,—that of our ministration. The Gospel record tells us (Mt 17:2-4) that Christ clearly revealed such glory to his disciples when his face shone as the sun, and Moses and Elijah were present. Before the manifestation of such glory, the disciples did not flee; they beheld with amazed joy and said: "Lord, it is good for us to be here. We will make here tabernacles for thee and for Moses," etc.

50. Compare the two scenes and you will understand plainly the import of Paul's words here. As before said, this is the substance of his meaning: "The Law produces naught but terror and death when it dazzles the heart with its glory and stands revealed in its true nature. On the other hand, the Gospel yields comfort and joy." But to explain in detail the signification of the veiled face of Moses, and of his shining uncovered face, would take too long to enter

upon here.

51. There is also especial comfort to be derived from Paul's assertion that the "ministration," or doctrine, of the Law "passeth away"; for otherwise there would be naught but eternal condemnation. The doctrine of the Law "passes away" when the preaching of the Gospel of Christ finds place. To Christ, Moses shall yield, that he alone may hold sway. Moses shall not terrify the conscience of the believer. When, perceiving the glory of Moses, the conscience trembles and despairs before God's wrath, then it is time for Christ's glory to shine with its gracious, comforting light into the heart. Then can the heart endure Moses and Elijah. For the glory of the Law, or the unveiled face of Moses, shall shine only until man is humbled and driven to desire the blessed countenance of Christ. If you come to Christ, you shall no longer hear Moses to your fright and terror; you shall hear him as one who remains servant to the Lord Christ, leaving the solace and the joy of his countenance unobscured. In conclusion:

"For verily that which hath been made glorious hath not been made glorious in this respect, by reason of the glory that surpasseth."

52. The meaning here is; When the glory and holiness of Christ, revealed through the preaching of the Gospel, is rightly perceived then the glory of the Law—which is but a feeble and transitory glory—is seen to be not really glorious. It is mere dark clouds in contrast to the light of Christ shining to lead us out of sin, death and hell unto God and eternal life.

The Parable of the Sower

The Disciples & the Fruits of God's Word

LUKE 8:4-15: And when much people were gathered together, and were come to him out of every city, he spake by a parable: A sower went out to sow his seed: and as he sowed, some fell by the way side; and it was trodden down, and the fowls of the air devoured it. And some fell upon a rock; and as soon as it was sprung up, it withered away, because it lacked moisture. And some fell among thorns; and the thorns sprang up with it, and choked it. And other fell on good ground, and sprang up, and bare fruit an hundredfold. And when he had said these things, he cried, He that hath ears to hear, let him hear. And his disciples asked him, saying, What might this parable be? And he said, Unto you it is given to know the mysteries of the kingdom of God: but to others in parables; that seeing they might not see, and hearing they might not understand. Now the parable is this: The seed is the word of God. Those by the way side are they that hear; then cometh the devil, and taketh away the word out of their hearts, lest they should believe and be saved. They on the rock are they, which, when they hear, receive the word with joy; and these have no root, which for a while believe, and in time of temptation fall away. And that which fell among thorns are they, which, when they have heard, go forth, and are choked with cares and riches and pleasures of this life, and bring no fruit to perfection. But that on the good ground are they, which in an honest and good heart, having heard the word, keep it, and bring forth fruit with patience..

Section I. the Nature of the Word Spoken Here.

1. This Gospel treats of the disciples and the fruits, which the Word of God develops in the world. It does not speak of the law nor of human institutions; but, as Christ himself says, of the Word of God, which he himself the sower preaches, for the law bears no fruit, just as little as do the institutions of men. Christ however sets forth here four kinds of disciples of the divine Word.

Section II. The Disciples of this Word.

2. The first class of disciples are those who hear the Word but neither understand nor esteem it. And these are not the mean people in the world, but

the greatest, wisest and the most saintly, in short they are the greatest part of mankind; for Christ does not speak here of those who persecute the Word nor of those who fail to give their ear to it, but of those who hear it and are students of it, who also wish to be called true Christians and to live in Christian fellowship with Christians and are partakers of baptism and the Lord's Supper. But they are of a carnal heart, and remain so, failing to appropriate the Word of God to themselves, it goes in one ear and out the other. Just like the seed along the wayside did not fall into the earth, but remained lying on the ground in the wayside, because the road was tramped hard by the feet of man and beast and it could not take root.

3. Therefore Christ says the devil cometh and taketh away the Word from their heart, that they may not believe and be saved. What power of Satan this alone reveals, that hearts, hardened through a worldly mind and life, lose the Word and let it go, so that they never understand or confess it; but instead of the Word of God Satan sends false teachers to tread it under foot by the doctrines of men. For it stands here written both that it was trodden under foot, and the birds of the heaven devoured it. The birds Christ himself interprets as the messengers of the devil, who snatch away the Word and devour it, which is done when he turns and blinds their hearts so that they neither understand nor esteem it, as St. Paul says in 2 Tim 4:4: "They will turn away their ears from the truth, and turn aside unto fables." By the treading under foot of men Christ means the teachings of men, that rule in our hearts, as he says in Mt 5:13 also of the salt that has lost its savor, it is cast out and trodden under foot, of men; that is, as St. Paul says in 2 Ths. 2:11, they must believe a lie because they have not been obedient to the truth.

4. Thus all heretics, fanatics and sects belong to this number, who understand the Gospel in a carnal way and explain it as they please, to suit their own ideas, all of whom hear the Gospel and yet they bear no fruit, yea, more, they are governed by Satan and are harder oppressed by human institutions than they were before they heard the Word. For it is a dreadful utterance that Christ here gives that the devil taketh away the Word from their hearts, by which he clearly proves that the devil rules mightily in their hearts, notwithstanding they are called Christians and hear the Word. Likewise it sounds terribly that they are to be trodden under foot, and must be subject unto men and to their ruinous teachings, by which under the appearance and name of the Gospel the devil takes the Word from them, so that they may never believe and be saved, but must be lost forever; as the fanatical spirits of our day do in all lands. For where this Word is not, there is no salvation, and great works or holy lives avail nothing, for [it is] with this, that he says: "They shall not be saved," since they have not the Word, he shows forcibly enough, that not their works but their faith in the Word alone saves, as Paul says to the Romans: "It is, the power of God unto salvation to every one that believeth" (Rom 1:16).

5. The second class of hearers are those who receive the Word with joy, but

they do not persevere. These are also a large multitude who understand the Word correctly and lay hold of it in its purity without any spirit of sect, division or fanaticism, they rejoice also in that they know the real truth, and are able to know how they may be saved without works through faith. They also know that they are free from the bondage of the law, of their conscience and of human teachings; but when it comes to the test that they must suffer harm, disgrace and loss of life or property, then they fall and deny it; for they have not root enough, and are not planted deep enough in the soil. Hence they are like the growth on a rock, which springs forth fresh and green, that it is a pleasure to behold it and it awakens bright hopes. But when the sun shines hot it withers, because it has no soil and moisture, and only rock is there. So these do; in times of persecution they deny or keep silence about the Word, and work, speak and suffer all that their persecutors mention or wish, who formerly went forth and spoke, and confessed with a fresh and joyful spirit the same, while there was still peace and no heat, so that there was hope they would bear much fruit and serve the people. For these fruits are not only the works, but more the confession, preaching and spreading of the Word, so that many others may thereby be converted and the kingdom of God be developed.

6. The third class are those who hear and understand the Word, but still it falls on the other side of the road, among the pleasures and cares of this life, so that they also do nothing with the Word. And there is quite a large multitude of these; for although they do not start heresies, like the first, but always possess the absolutely pure Word, they are also, not attacked on the left as the others with opposition and persecution; yet they fall on the right side, and it is their ruin that they enjoy peace and good days. Therefore they do not earnestly give themselves to the Word, but become indifferent and sink in the cares, riches and pleasures of this life, so that they are of no benefit to any one. Therefore they are like the seed that fell among the thorns. Although it is not rocky but good soil; not wayside but deeply plowed soil; yet, the thorns will not let it spring up, they choke it. Thus these have all in the Word that is needed for their salvation, but they do not make any use of it, and they rot in this life in carnal pleasures. To these belong those who hear the Word but do not bring under subjection their flesh. They know their duty but do it not, they teach but do not practice what they teach, and are this year as they were last.

7. The fourth class are those who lay hold of and keep the Word in a good and honest heart, and bring forth fruit with patience, those who hear the Word and steadfastly retain it, meditate upon it and act in harmony with it. The devil does not snatch it away, nor are they thereby led astray, moreover the heat of persecution does not rob them of it, and the thorns of pleasure and the avarice of the times do not hinder its growth; but they bear fruit by teaching others and by developing the kingdom of God, hence they also do good to their neighbor in love; and therefore Christ adds, "they bring forth fruit with patience." For these must suffer much on account of the Word, shame and disgrace from fanatics

and heretics, hatred and jealousy with injury to body and property from their persecutors, not to mention what the thorns and the temptations of their own flesh do, so that it may well be called the Word of the cross; for he who would keep it must bear the cross and misfortune, and triumph. field,

8. He says: "In honest and good hearts." Like a field that is without a thorn or brush, cleared and spacious, as a beautiful clean place: so a heart is also cleared and clean, broad and spacious, that is without cares and avarice as to temporal needs, so that the Word of God truly finds lodgment there. But the field is good, not only when it lies there cleared and level, but when it is also rich and fruitful, possesses soil and is productive, and not like a stony and gravelly field. Just so is the heart that has good soil and with a full spirit is strong, fertile and good to keep the Word and bring forth fruit with patience.

9. Here we see why it is no wonder there are so few true Christians, for all the seed does not fall into good ground, but only the fourth and small part; and that they are not to be trusted who boast they are Christians and praise the teaching of the Gospel; like Demas, a disciple of St. Paul, who forsook him at last (2 Tim. 4:10); like the disciples of Jesus, who turned their backs to him (John 6:66). For Christ himself cries out here: "He that hath ears to hear, let him hear," as if he should say: O, how few true Christians there are; one dare not believe all to be Christians who are called Christians and hear the Gospel, more is required than that.

10. All this is spoken for our instruction, that we may not go astray, since so many misuse the Gospel and few lay hold of it aright. True it is unpleasant to preach to those who treat the Gospel so shamefully and even oppose it. For preaching is to become so universal that the Gospel is to be proclaimed to all creatures, as Christ says in Mk. 16:15: "Preach the Gospel to the whole creation;" and Ps. 19:4: "Their line is gone out through all the earth, and their words to the end of the world." What business is it of mine that many do not esteem it? It must be that many are called but few are chosen. For the sake of the good ground that brings forth fruit with patience, the seed must also fall fruitless by the wayside, on the rock and among the thorns; inasmuch as we are assured that the Word of God does not go forth without bearing some fruit, but it always finds also good ground; as Christ says here, some seed of the sower falls also into good ground, and not only by the wayside, among the thorns and on stony ground. For wherever the Gospel goes you will find Christians. "My word shall not return unto me void" (Is. 55:11).

Section IV. Why Christ Calls the Doctrine Concerning the Disciples and the Fruits of the Word a Mystery.

19. But what does it mean when he says: "Unto you it is given to know the mysteries of the kingdom of God", etc.? What are the mysteries? Shall one not

know them, why then are they preached? A "mystery" is a hidden secret, that is not known: and the "mysteries of the kingdom of God" are the things in the kingdom of God, as for example Christ with all his grace, which he manifests to us, as Paul describes him; for he who knows Christ aright understands what God's kingdom is, and what is in it. And it is called a mystery because it is spiritual and secret, and indeed it remains so, where the spirit does not reveal it. For although there are many who see and hear it, yet they do not understand it. just as there are many who preach and hear Christ, how he offered himself for us; but all that is only upon their tongue and not in their heart; for they themselves do not believe it, they do not experience it, as Paul in 1 Cor. 2:14 says: "The natural man receiveth not the things of the Spirit of God!" Therefore Christ says here: "Unto you it is given", the Spirit gives it to you that you not only hear and see it, but acknowledge and believe it with your heart. Therefore it is now no longer a mystery to you. But to the others who hear it as well as you, and have no faith in their heart, they see and understand it not; to them it is a mystery and it will continue unknown to them, and all that they hear is only like one hearing a parable or a dark saying. This is also proved by the fanatics of our day, who know so much to preach about Christ; but as they themselves do not experience it in their heart, they rush ahead and pass by the true foundation of the mystery and tramp around with questions and rare foundlings, and when it comes to the test they do not know the least thing about trusting in God and finding in Christ the forgiveness of their sins.

20. But Mark says (4:33), Christ spake therefore to the people with parables, that they might understand, each according to his ability. How does that agree with what Matthew says, 13:13-14: He spake therefore unto them in parables, because they did not understand? It must surely be that Mark wishes to say that parables serve to the end that they may get a hold of coarse, rough people, although they do not indeed understand them, yet later, they may be taught and then they know: for parables are naturally pleasing to the common people, and they easily remember them since they are taken from common every day affairs, in the midst of which the people live. But Matthew means to say that these parables are of the nature that no one can understand them, they may grasp and hear them as often as they will, unless the Spirit makes them known and reveals them. Not that they should preach that we shall not understand them; but it naturally follows that wherever the Spirit does not reveal them, no one understands them. However, Christ took these words from Is. 6:9-10, where the high meaning of the divine foreknowledge is referred to, that God conceals and reveals to whom he will and whom he had in mind from eternity.

Martin Luther's Ninety-Five Theses

October 31, 1517

Disputation of Doctor Martin Luther on the Power and Efficacy of Indulgences

Out of love for the truth and the desire to bring it to light, the following propositions will be discussed at Wittenberg, under the presidency of the Reverend Father Martin Luther, Master of Arts and of Sacred Theology, and Lecturer in Ordinary on the same at that place. Wherefore he requests that those who are unable to be present and debate orally with us, may do so by letter.

In the Name our Lord Jesus Christ. Amen.

1. Our Lord and Master Jesus Christ, when He said Poenitentiam agite, willed that the whole life of believers should be repentance.

2. This word cannot be understood to mean sacramental penance, i.e., confession and satisfaction, which is administered by the priests.

3. Yet it means not inward repentance only; nay, there is no inward repentance which does not outwardly work divers mortifications of the flesh.

4. The penalty [of sin], therefore, continues so long as hatred of self continues; for this is the true inward repentance, and continues until our entrance into the kingdom of heaven.

5. The pope does not intend to remit, and cannot remit any penalties other than those which he has imposed either by his own authority or by that of the Canons.

6. The pope cannot remit any guilt, except by declaring that it has been remitted by God and by assenting to God's remission; though, to be sure, he may grant remission in cases reserved to his judgment. If his right to grant remission in such cases were despised, the guilt would remain entirely unforgiven.

7. God remits guilt to no one whom He does not, at the same time, humble in all things and bring into subjection to His vicar, the priest. 8. The penitential

canons are imposed only on the living, and, according to them, nothing should be imposed on the dying.

9. Therefore the Holy Spirit in the pope is kind to us, because in his decrees he always makes exception of the article of death and of necessity.

10. Ignorant and wicked are the doings of those priests who, in the case of the dying, reserve canonical penances for purgatory.

11. This changing of the canonical penalty to the penalty of purgatory is quite evidently one of the tares that were sown while the bishops slept.

12. In former times the canonical penalties were imposed not after, but before absolution, as tests of true contrition.

13. The dying are freed by death from all penalties; they are already dead to canonical rules, and have a right to be released from them.

14. The imperfect health [of soul], that is to say, the imperfect love, of the dying brings with it, of necessity, great fear; and the smaller the love, the greater is the fear.

15. This fear and horror is sufficient of itself alone (to say nothing of other things) to constitute the penalty of purgatory, since it is very near to the horror of despair.

16. Hell, purgatory, and heaven seem to differ as do despair, almost-despair, and the assurance of safety.

17. With souls in purgatory it seems necessary that horror should grow less and love increase.

18. It seems unproved, either by reason or Scripture, that they are outside the state of merit, that is to say, of increasing love.

19. Again, it seems unproved that they, or at least that all of them, are certain or assured of their own blessedness, though we may be quite certain of it.

20. Therefore by "full remission of all penalties" the pope means not actually "of all," but only of those imposed by himself.

21. Therefore those preachers of indulgences are in error, who say that by the pope's indulgences a man is freed from every penalty, and saved;

22. Whereas he remits to souls in purgatory no penalty which, according to the canons, they would have had to pay in this life. 23. If it is at all possible to grant to any one the remission of all penalties whatsoever, it is certain that this remission can be granted only to the most perfect, that is, to the very fewest.

24. It must needs be, therefore, that the greater part of the people are deceived by that indiscriminate and highsounding promise of release from penalty.

25. The power which the pope has, in a general way, over purgatory, is just like the power which any bishop or curate has, in a special way, within his own diocese or parish.

26. The pope does well when he grants remission to souls [in purgatory], not by the power of the keys (which he does not possess), but by way of intercession.

27. They preach man who say that so soon as the penny jingles into the money-box, the soul flies out [of purgatory].

28. It is certain that when the penny jingles into the money-box, gain and avarice can be increased, but the result of the intercession of the Church is in the power of God alone.

29. Who knows whether all the souls in purgatory wish to be bought out of it, as in the legend of Sts. Severinus and Paschal.

30. No one is sure that his own contrition is sincere; much less that he has attained full remission.

31. Rare as is the man that is truly penitent, so rare is also the man who truly buys indulgences, i.e., such men are most rare.

32. They will be condemned eternally, together with their teachers, who believe themselves sure of their salvation because they have letters of pardon.

33. Men must be on their guard against those who say that the pope's pardons are that inestimable gift of God by which man is reconciled to Him;

34. For these "graces of pardon" concern only the penalties of sacramental satisfaction, and these are appointed by man.

35. They preach no Christian doctrine who teach that contrition is not necessary in those who intend to buy souls out of purgatory or to buy confessionalia.

36. Every truly repentant Christian has a right to full remission of penalty and guilt, even without letters of pardon.

37. Every true Christian, whether living or dead, has part in all the blessings of Christ and the Church; and this is granted him by God, even without letters of pardon.

38. Nevertheless, the remission and participation [in the blessings of the Church] which are granted by the pope are in no way to be despised, for they are, as I have said, the declaration of divine remission.

39. It is most difficult, even for the very keenest theologians, at one and the same time to commend to the people the abundance of pardons and [the need of] true contrition.

40. True contrition seeks and loves penalties, but liberal pardons only relax penalties and cause them to be hated, or at least, furnish an occasion [for hating them].

41. Apostolic pardons are to be preached with caution, lest the people may falsely think them preferable to other good works of love.

42. Christians are to be taught that the pope does not intend the buying of

pardons to be compared in any way to works of mercy.

43. Christians are to be taught that he who gives to the poor or lends to the needy does a better work than buying pardons;

44. Because love grows by works of love, and man becomes better; but by pardons man does not grow better, only more free from penalty.

45. Christians are to be taught that he who sees a man in need, and passes him by, and gives [his money] for pardons, purchases not the indulgences of the pope, but the indignation of God.

46. Christians are to be taught that unless they have more than they need, they are bound to keep back what is necessary for their own families, and by no means to squander it on pardons.

47. Christians are to be taught that the buying of pardons is a matter of free will, and not of commandment.

48. Christians are to be taught that the pope, in granting pardons, needs, and therefore desires, their devout prayer for him more than the money they bring.

49. Christians are to be taught that the pope's pardons are useful, if they do not put their trust in them; but altogether harmful, if through them they lose their fear of God.

50. Christians are to be taught that if the pope knew the exactions of the pardon-preachers, he would rather that St. Peter's church should go to ashes, than that it should be built up with the skin, flesh and bones of his sheep.

51. Christians are to be taught that it would be the pope's wish, as it is his duty, to give of his own money to very many of those from whom certain hawkers of pardons cajole money, even though the church of St. Peter might have to be sold.

52. The assurance of salvation by letters of pardon is vain, even though the commissary, nay, even though the pope himself, were to stake his soul upon it.

53. They are enemies of Christ and of the pope, who bid the Word of God be altogether silent in some Churches, in order that pardons may be preached in others.

54. Injury is done the Word of God when, in the same sermon, an equal or a longer time is spent on pardons than on this Word.

55. It must be the intention of the pope that if pardons, which are a very small thing, are celebrated with one bell, with single processions and ceremonies, then the Gospel, which is the very greatest thing, should be preached with a hundred bells, a hundred processions, a hundred ceremonies.

56. The "treasures of the Church," out of which the pope. grants indulgences, are not sufficiently named or known among the people of Christ.

57. That they are not temporal treasures is certainly evident, for many of the vendors do not pour out such treasures so easily, but only gather them.

58. Nor are they the merits of Christ and the Saints, for even without the pope, these always work grace for the inner man, and the cross, death, and hell for the outward man.

59. St. Lawrence said that the treasures of the Church were the Church's poor, but he spoke according to the usage of the word in his own time.

60. Without rashness we say that the keys of the Church, given by Christ's merit, are that treasure;

61. For it is clear that for the remission of penalties and of reserved cases, the power of the pope is of itself sufficient.

62. The true treasure of the Church is the Most Holy Gospel of the glory and the grace of God.

63. But this treasure is naturally most odious, for it makes the first to be last.

64. On the other hand, the treasure of indulgences is naturally most acceptable, for it makes the last to be first.

65. Therefore the treasures of the Gospel are nets with which they formerly were wont to fish for men of riches.

66. The treasures of the indulgences are nets with which they now fish for the riches of men.

67. The indulgences which the preachers cry as the "greatest graces" are known to be truly such, in so far as they promote gain.

68. Yet they are in truth the very smallest graces compared with the grace of God and the piety of the Cross.

69. Bishops and curates are bound to admit the commissaries of apostolic pardons, with all reverence.

70. But still more are they bound to strain all their eyes and attend with all their ears, lest these men preach their own dreams instead of the commission of the pope.

71 . He who speaks against the truth of apostolic pardons, let him be anathema and accursed!

72. But he who guards against the lust and license of the pardon-preachers, let him be blessed!

73. The pope justly thunders against those who, by any art, contrive the injury of the traffic in pardons.

74. But much more does he intend to thunder against those who use the pretext of pardons to contrive the injury of holy love and truth.

75. To think the papal pardons so great that they could absolve a man even if he had committed an impossible sin and violated the Mother of God — this is madness.

76. We say, on the contrary, that the papal pardons are not able to remove the

very least of venial sins, so far as its guilt is concerned.

77. It is said that even St. Peter, if he were now Pope, could not bestow greater graces; this is blasphemy against St. Peter and against the pope.

78. We say, on the contrary, that even the present pope, and any pope at all, has greater graces at his disposal; to wit, the Gospel, powers, gifts of healing, etc., as it is written in I. Corinthians xii.

79. To say that the cross, emblazoned with the papal arms, which is set up [by the preachers of indulgences], is of equal worth with the Cross of Christ, is blasphemy.

80. The bishops, curates and theologians who allow such talk to be spread among the people, will have an account to render. 81. This unbridled preaching of pardons makes it no easy matter, even for learned men, to rescue the reverence due to the pope from slander, or even from the shrewd questionings of the laity.

82. To wit: — "Why does not the pope empty purgatory, for the sake of holy love and of the dire need of the souls that are there, if he redeems an infinite number of souls for the sake of miserable money with which to build a Church? The former reasons would be most just; the latter is most trivial."

83. Again: — "Why are mortuary and anniversary masses for the dead continued, and why does he not return or permit the withdrawal of the endowments founded on their behalf, since it is wrong to pray for the redeemed?"

84. Again: — "What is this new piety of God and the pope, that for money they allow a man who is impious and their enemy to buy out of purgatory the pious soul of a friend of God, and do not rather, because of that pious and beloved soul's own need, free it for pure love's sake?"

85. Again: — "Why are the penitential canons long since in actual fact and through disuse abrogated and dead, now satisfied by the granting of indulgences, as though they were still alive and in force?"

86. Again: — "Why does not the pope, whose wealth is to-day greater than the riches of the richest, build just this one church of St. Peter with his own money, rather than with the money of poor believers?"

87. Again: — "What is it that the pope remits, and what participation does he grant to those who, by perfect contrition, have a right to full remission and participation?"

88. Again: — "What greater blessing could come to the Church than if the pope were to do a hundred times a day what he now does once, and bestow on every believer these remissions and participations?"

89. "Since the pope, by his pardons, seeks the salvation of souls rather than money, why does he suspend the indulgences and pardons granted heretofore, since these have equal efficacy?"

90. To repress these arguments and scruples of the laity by force alone, and not to resolve them by giving reasons, is to expose the Church and the pope to the ridicule of their enemies, and to make Christians unhappy.

91. If, therefore, pardons were preached according to the spirit and mind of the pope, all these doubts would be readily resolved; nay, they would not exist.

92. Away, then, with all those prophets who say to the people of Christ, "Peace, peace," and there is no peace!

93. Blessed be all those prophets who say to the people of Christ, "Cross, cross," and there is no cross!

94. Christians are to be exhorted that they be diligent in following Christ, their Head, through penalties, deaths, and hell;

95. And thus be confident of entering into heaven rather through many tribulations, than through the assurance of peace.

www.ingramcontent.com/pod-product-compliance
Lightning Source LLC
LaVergne TN
LVHW011331080426
835513LV00006B/286